SECOND GRADE SKILLS

Thinking Kids®
Carson-Dellosa Publishing LLC
Greensboro, North Carolina

Thinking Kids®
Carson-Dellosa Publishing LLC
PO Box 35665
Greensboro, NC 27425 USA

ISBN 978-1-4838-4117-5

Contents

Letter to Parents & Caregivers 4

Checklist of Essential Second Grade Skills 5

Phonics & Spelling 6–43
Beginning & Ending Consonants • Consonant Blends & Digraphs • Spelling Patterns
• Short & Long Vowels • Syllables

Vocabulary 44–79
Sight Words • Context Clues • Classifying Words • Prefixes, Suffixes, & Base Words
• Shades of Meaning • Compound Words • Dictionary Skills

Language Arts 80–111
Grammar Review • Collective Nouns • Irregular Plurals • Reflexive Pronouns • Irregular
Verbs • Adjectives & Adverbs • Expanding & Combining Sentences
• Capitalization • Commas • Contractions & Possessives

Reading Comprehension 112–123
Sequencing • Classifying • Comparing & Contrasting • Fact & Opinion • Predicting
• Answering Questions

Writing 124–135
Writing a Story • Writing to Inform • Writing an Opinion

Math Skills to 100 136–159
Addition & Subtraction • Word Problems • Counting by Twos • Odd & Even Numbers
• Arrays

Math Skills to 1,000 160–205
Place Value • Expanded Form • Writing Number Names • Comparing Numbers •
Counting by Ones, Fives, Tens, & Hundreds • Addition & Subtraction • Word Problems

Measurement & Data 206–259
Measuring Length • Using Number Lines • Telling Time • Counting Money • Making Graphs

Shapes 260–275
Classifying Flat & Solid Shapes • Quadrilaterals • Drawing Shapes • Partitioning Shapes
• Equal Shares: Halves, Fourths, & Thirds

Answer Key 276–320

Dear Parents & Caregivers

Dear Parents and Caregivers,

Welcome to *Second Grade Skills!* Inside this comprehensive resource, you'll find an abundance of joyful, child-centered learning activities that will guide your child step-by-step as he or she explores these essential skills for school success:

Reading & Writing Skills: Your child will gain practice with phonics, spelling, parts of speech, types of sentences, contractions, and possessives. He or she will develop reading comprehension skills and write stories, informational reports, and opinions.

Vocabulary Development: Your child will recognize words by sight, learn to use a dictionary, and determine word meanings based on context clues, prefixes and suffixes, compound words, and more.

Math Skills: Your child will add and subtract within 1,000, work with place value, and begin to learn the fundamentals of multiplication and fractions.

Applying Math Skills: Your child will measure length, tell time, count money, make graphs, and classify shapes.

While academics are important, social and emotional skills also play a huge role in school success. Throughout this book, you and your child will find fun activities and practical tips that promote development in these vital areas:

everything that makes your child special and unique

healthy eating, exercise, safety, and more

making friends and getting along with others

honesty, responsibility, tolerance, and more

effort and attitude as the keys to learning and growth

So, invite your child to grab a pencil and get going! Over 250 fun and educational activities are at your fingertips!

Sincerely,
Thinking Kids®

Essential Second Grade Skills

Reading & Writing Skills:
I can…

- ❑ associate sounds and letters in order to read and spell two-syllable words.
- ❑ understand nouns and pronouns.
- ❑ use verbs, including irregular verbs, correctly in sentences.
- ❑ use adjectives and adverbs to expand sentences.
- ❑ combine simple sentences into compound sentences.
- ❑ use apostrophes in contractions and possessives.
- ❑ use a dictionary to find spellings and word meanings.
- ❑ read many words by sight.
- ❑ use context clues and knowledge of prefixes and suffixes to find word meanings.
- ❑ answer questions about what I read.
- ❑ write stories, facts, and opinions.

Math Skills: I can…

- ❑ count by twos, fives, tens, and hundreds to 1,000.
- ❑ identify odd and even numbers.
- ❑ count objects in rectangular arrays.
- ❑ use place value to compare three-digit numbers and write them in standard and expanded forms.
- ❑ add and subtract within 1,000.
- ❑ measure in inches, feet, centimeters, and meters.
- ❑ use a number line to solve problems.
- ❑ tell time to the nearest five minutes.
- ❑ count coins and dollar bills.
- ❑ make and interpret line plots, picture graphs, and bar graphs.
- ❑ use attributes to classify flat and solid shapes.
- ❑ understand halves, fourths, and thirds.

Motor Skills: I can…

- ❑ manipulate buttons, zippers, and shoelaces.
- ❑ better control handwriting and cutting with scissors.
- ❑ jump over an object, landing with both of my feet together.
- ❑ catch a small ball using my hands only.
- ❑ walk on a balance beam.
- ❑ walk backward.
- ❑ balance and hop on one foot.

Social/Emotional Skills: I can…

- ❑ find joy in being part of a team, group, or club.
- ❑ respect others and the rights of others.
- ❑ describe my thoughts and feelings.
- ❑ follow classroom rules and routines.
- ❑ start seeing things from other points of view and respond to others with sensitivity.
- ❑ express my opinions more freely, even when they don't align with the views of my peers.
- ❑ apologize when I am wrong.

Beginning Consonants

Write the beginning consonant for each word.

_____ox

_____at

_____oat

_____ouse

_____og

_____ire

Beginning Consonants

Write the beginning consonant for each word.

_____oney

_____acket

_____ion

_____an

_____ey

_____ose

Beginning Consonants

Say the name of each picture. Circle the letter that makes its beginning sound.

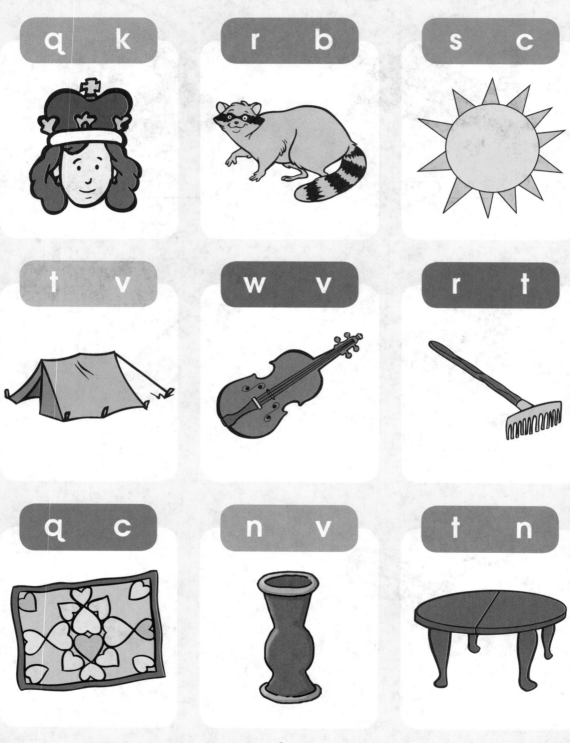

q k   r b   s c

t v   w v   r t

q c   n v   t n

8

Beginning Consonants

Draw a line from each letter to the picture whose name begins with the sound it makes.

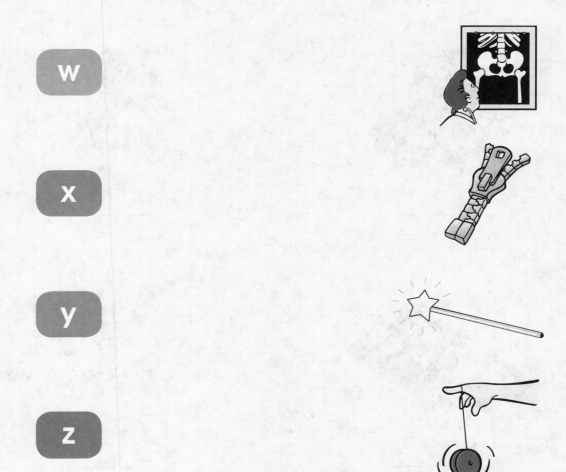

w

x

y

z

You hear the **consonant** sound **x** in **excuse**. Think about each situation. Check the box if you should say, "Excuse me."

☐ You want to get someone's attention.

☐ You burp or make a rude noise.

☐ You didn't hear what someone said.

☐ You bump into someone.

Ending Consonants

Write the ending consonant for each word.

fro_____

cu_____

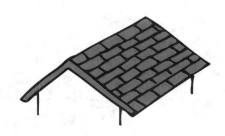

roo_____

do_____

be_____

bi_____

Ending Consonants

Say the name of each picture. Circle the letter that makes its ending sound.

l   n

n   m

m   e

t   n

x   s

k   p

l   m

m   n

t   n

11

Consonant Blends & Digraphs

Say the name of each picture. Write the consonant blend or digraph you hear at the beginning of the word.

___ ___apes

___ ___elf

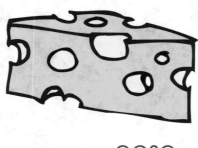

___ ___eese

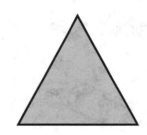

___ ___iangle

___ ___ow

___ ___ale

Consonant Blends & Digraphs

Say the name of each picture. Write the consonant blend or digraph you hear at the beginning of the word.

___ ___unk

___ ___ag

___ ___oom

___ ___umb

Three **consonants** blend at the beginning of **strong**. It is important to keep your muscles strong and healthy. Check at least one way you will try to build strength.

☐ Do cartwheels.

☐ Do push-ups.

☐ Walk on your hands and feet like a crab.

☐ Squat, jump straight up, repeat.

☐ Do handstands against a wall.

Health & Fitness

Consonant Blends & Digraphs

Write a word to name each picture. Find at least one consonant blend or digraph in each word you write.

skate	whistle	plate	fly	ship
flower	snake	thimble		chicken

_____

_____

_____

_____

_____

_____

_____

_____

_____

Consonant Blends & Digraphs

Write a word to name each picture. Find at least one consonant blend or digraph in each word you write.

peach	trash	branch	teeth	slide
crocodile	match	bench	whiskers	

_____

_____

_____

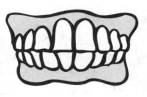

_____

_____

_____

_____

_____

_____

15

Consonant Blends & Digraphs

Write words to answer the riddles. Find at least one consonant blend or digraph in each word you write.

| which | glass | splash | sleep |

This word has **s-e-e**, but it names something you do when your eyes are closed.

What is it? _____

This word names something you can find in a window or in your cupboard.

What is it? _____

The letters in the middle of this word spell **hi**. You use it when you think about making a choice.

What is it? _____

This word names a sound.

What is it? _____

Consonant Blends & Digraphs

Write words to answer the riddles. Find at least one consonant blend or digraph in each word you write.

| trash | blow | beach | glove |

This word has **l-o-v-e**. It names something your hand loves on a cold day.

What is it? _____

This word is a verb that tells what to do to make a bubble.

What is it? _____

This word names a place where castles stand for only one day.

What is it? _____

This word names something that no one wants.

What is it? _____

Double Consonants

To spell some words, double the consonant in the middle of the word. Write words to match the pictures and complete the puzzles. In each word you write, double the consonant shown.

Double Consonants

To spell some words, double the consonant in the middle of the word. Write words to match the pictures and complete the puzzles. In each word you write, double the consonant shown.

There is a **double consonant** in **hobby**. Circle something that represents a hobby you enjoy or draw something on your own.

All About Me

Silent Consonants

Some words have consonants that you cannot hear at all, such as **gh** in **night**, **w** in **wrong**, and **l** in **walk**. Write a word to name each picture. Underline at least one silent consonant in each word you write.

wrench   comb   eight   lamb   wrist   calf

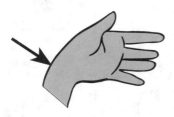

_____

_____

_____

_____

_____

Silent Consonants

Write a word to name each picture. Underline at least one silent consonant in each word you write.

| knee | thumb | light | knife | whistle | knob |

_____

_____

_____

_____

_____

_____

21

Hard & Soft c

When **c** is followed by **e**, **i**, or **y**, it usually has a soft sound, like the **c** in **pencil**. When **c** is followed by **a**, **o**, or **u**, it usually has a hard sound, like the **c** in **cat**. Say each word. If it has a soft **c** sound, write it under the pencil. If it has a hard **c** sound, write it under the cat.

dance	carrot	cent	card
popcorn	cookie	mice	rice

pencil

cat

_____   _____

_____   _____

_____   _____

_____   _____

Hard & Soft g

When **g** is followed by **e**, **i**, or **y**, it usually has a soft sound, like the **g** in **giraffe**. When **g** is followed by **a**, **o**, or **u**, it usually has a hard sound, like the **g** in **gate**. Say each word. If it has a soft **g** sound, write it under the giraffe. If it has a hard **g** sound, write it under the gate.

| engine | garden | cage | magic |
| giant | goes | gum | goal |

giraffe

gate

_____

_____

_____

_____

_____

_____

_____

_____

23

Short Vowels

Say the name of each picture. Complete the word by writing the letter that spells the short vowel sound.

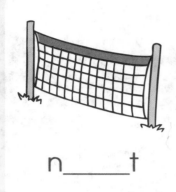

n____t

s____ck

l____ps

b____ttle

p____p

l____dder

h____t

p____nny

p____n

Short Vowels

Say the name of each picture. Complete the word by writing the letter that spells the short vowel sound.

_____x

p_____pcorn

t_____nt

th_____mble

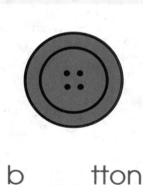

b_____tton

f_____x

h_____mmer

p_____ppet

c_____ndle

Super Silent e

Super silent **e** changes short vowel sounds into long vowel sounds! Read each word that has a short vowel sound. Next, write silent **e** at the end of the word. Then, read the new word you made. Do you hear the long vowel sound?

can___   rob___   cub___

slid___   tap___   bit___

cap___   fin___   dim___

Mistake has the long **a** sound. It ends with silent **e**. Everyone makes mistakes! When you make a mistake, do not feel bad about yourself or give up. Instead, think about what you can learn from your mistake and how you can do better next time.

Growth Mindset

Vowel Teams

Long vowel sounds are often spelled by two vowels together, or vowel teams. Unscramble and write each word. Circle the vowel team.

____ ____ ____ ____
e   s   d   e

____ ____ ____ ____
e   f   t   e

____ ____ ____ ____
i   p   a   l

____ ____ ____ ____
a   s   t   e

____ ____ ____ ____
g   t   a   o

____ ____ ____ ____
l   a   s   i

27

Vowel Teams

In words with vowel teams, the first vowel letter often says its name, or makes a long vowel sound. The second vowel letter is silent. Read each long vowel word. Circle the vowel that makes the long vowel sound. Draw a box around the vowel that is silent.

t e a r

b o a t

p e a s

m e a t

c o a t

r a i n

The long **a** sound in **wait** is spelled with the vowel team **ai**. When you have something to say, it can be hard to wait for your turn to talk. Check one way you will try to not interrupt.

- [ ] Be interested in what others say. Make sure you understand their ideas.

- [ ] Patiently raise your hand or use another signal to show that you have something to say.

- [ ] In a group, pass around a toy or another object. When someone is holding the toy, everyone else must listen. Make sure everyone has a turn.

Social Skills

Long a Spellings

Read each word. Write it under the letters that spell the long **a** sound.

| eight | plain | maze | basic | way |
| apron | sunray | waited | brave | weigh |

a

_____   _____

a-consonant-silent e

_____   _____

ay

_____   _____

ai

_____   _____

ei

_____   _____

29

Long e Spellings

Write a word to match each clue.

peace   greeting   complete
kneel   please

It has the long **e** sound spelled **ea**. It has a soft **c** sound.

_____

It has the long **e** sound spelled **e**-consonant-silent **e**. It has a consonant blend in the middle of the word.

_____

It has the long **e** sound spelled **ee**. It has a silent **k**.

_____

It has the long **e** sound spelled **ee**. It begins with a consonant blend.

_____

It has the long **e** sound spelled **ea**. It begins with a consonant blend.

_____

Long i Spellings

Read each word. Write it under the letters that spell the long **i** sound.

| tried | delight | silent | idea |
| side | lie | nice | tighten |

i

_____   _____

i-consonant-silent e

_____   _____

igh

_____   _____

ie

_____   _____

Long o Spellings

Write a word to match each clue.

broke   doe   below   road

It has the long **o** sound spelled **ow**.
It also has the long **e** sound.   _____

It has the long **o** sound spelled **oe**.
It means "a female deer."   _____

It has the long **o** sound spelled
o-consonant-silent **e**. It begins
with a consonant blend.   _____

It has the long **o** sound spelled **oa**.
It ends with the fourth letter
of the alphabet.   _____

You hear the long **o** sound at the end of **hero**. A hero is someone you look up to and respect. Finish the picture of your hero. Write about why you admire him or her.

My hero is _____.

This person is my hero because

_____

_____.

All About Me

Long u & Long oo Spellings

Read each word. Write it under the letters that spell the long **u** or long **oo** sound.

music	unit	flute	rude
blew	clue	new	dues

u

_____   _____

u-consonant-silent e

_____   _____

ue

_____   _____

ew

_____   _____

33

Short & Long Vowels

Write **Short** or **Long** to complete the description of the words in each box.

_____ Vowels

hose
take
bead
cube
eat
see

_____ Vowels

frog
hot
sled
lap
block
sit

_____ Vowels

cup
man
pet
fix
cat
pin

_____ Vowels

show
soap
seed
ice
rain
cake

Short & Long Vowels

Write the missing letters. Then, decide whether each word has a short vowel sound or a long vowel sound. Circle your choice.

long   short

k___t___

long   short

___pe

long   short

l___ck

long   short

h___s___

long   short

tr___ck

long   short

v___s___

long   short

l___ght

long   short

p___ach

long   short

l___ps

35

Syllables

Words can be divided into syllables. Each syllable has one vowel sound. The boxes below each word show how many syllables it has. Draw and color shapes in the boxes to show each syllable's vowel sound. Use the code.

- ● short a
- ○ long a
- ▲ short e
- ▲ long e
- ◆ short i
- ◆ long i

- ■ short o
- ■ long o
- ★ short u
- ★ long u or long oo

flag

pillow

smile

lunchbox

recess

crocodile

Syllables

Use the code from page 36. Match the words with the shapes that show their syllables and vowel sounds.

math

Sunday

rainbow

octopus

tree

basket

Y as a Vowel

Sometimes, **y** is a vowel. At the end of one-syllable words like **by** and **try**, the long **i** sound is spelled **y**. At the end of two-syllable words like **baby** and **lady**, the long **e** sound is spelled **y**. Read the word on each flag. If the word has long **i** spelled **y**, color the flag **red**. If the word has long **e** spelled **y**, color the flag **blue**.

sunny

rainy

sky

fly

dry

windy

Y as a Vowel

Say each word. If **y** spells the long **i** sound, write the word under **cry**. If **y** spells the long **e** sound, write the word under **baby**.

bunny	try	sleepy	funny
why	my	party	buy

cry   **baby**

_____   _____

_____   _____

_____   _____

_____   _____

The long **e** sound is spelled **y** at the end of **family**. Finish the sentence and draw a picture to show what your family likes to do together.

When we are together, my family likes to

_____

_____

_____

_____.

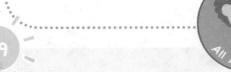

All About Me

R-Controlled Vowels

When a vowel is followed by the letter **r**, the vowel sound changes. Say **bid** and **bird**. Do you hear how **r** changes the short **i** sound? Complete each word and answer each riddle by writing a vowel letter followed by **r**.

I twinkle high in the sky.

What am I?   st_____

Use me with a knife.

What am I?   f_____k

I name a group of cows.

What am I?   h_____d

I am the opposite of tall.

What am I?   sh_____t

I have fields, a barn, and animals.

What am I?   f_____m

R-Controlled Vowels

Write a word with an **r**-controlled vowel to complete each sentence.

| bark | turtle | store | hurt | purple | dirt |

Our dog will _____ at anything that moves.

I bought a new toy at the _____.

We found ants in the _____.

A _____ is a reptile.

This shot may _____ a little.

Where is the _____ marker?

41

Special Vowel Teams

The vowel teams **ou** and **ow** can spell the same vowel sound. You hear it in **cloud** and **clown**. Write **ou** or **ow** to complete each word.

_____l

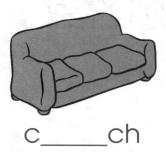

c_____ch

h_____se

t_____el

p_____der

m_____se

m_____th

h_____l

Special Vowel Teams

The vowel teams **oy** and **oi** can spell the same vowel sound. You hear it in **joy** and **foil**. Write **oy** or **oi** to complete each word.

b____l

t____s

b____

c____n

The vowel teams **au** and **aw** can spell the same vowel sound. You hear it in **because** and **law**. Write **au** or **aw** to complete each word.

____to

s____

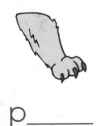

p____

s____ce

Sight Words: always & around

Write **always** or **around** to complete each sentence.

We _____ have a good time when we go to the swimming pool.

We usually arrive _____ one o'clock in the afternoon.

There are comfortable chairs all _____ the pool.

The water is _____ cold at first, but then it feels just right.

Always be safe **around** the water! Unscramble the words to complete the safety tips.

_____ around the pool.
lWka

Swim only when an adult is _____.
rena

Never _____ in shallow water.
eidv

Do not push others or hold them

_____ the water.
dneur

Sight Words: because & before

Circle **because** or **before** to complete each sentence.

We are playing inside today _____ it is raining.

because   before

Should we eat lunch _____ we begin the game?

because   before

Let's eat _____ the soup gets cold.

because   before

I want to play this game _____ we haven't played it in a long time.

because   before

45

Sight Words: been & best

Underline **been** or **best** in each sentence.

I like all fruits, but I like grapes the best.

Ben has been playing the violin since he was six.

The best thing about the beach is building sandcastles.

We have been playing baseball all day!

Sight Words: does & don't

Write **does** or **don't** to complete each sentence. Do not forget to put the apostrophe (') in the correct place each time you write **don't**.

Can you run as fast as Erin _____?

I _____ think so, but I can try!

_____ you want to play fetch, Baxter?

I bet Smokey _____! Let's go find him.

Write **does** or **don't** to complete each sentence about good friends.

A good friend _____ listen to you.

Good friends _____ brag and try to "one up" each other.

Good friends _____ say mean things about you.

A good friend _____ stick by you in good times and bad.

Social Skills

Sight Words: fast & first

Find and circle **fast** and **first** in the puzzle. Each word appears six times. Look across and down. Circle **fast** in **green**. Circle **first** in **blue**.

```
e f f i r s t w e w s
d u f l k o g c i f t
s i a h j f r x c b f
f a s t e r t f i r i
i e t o w l s a f i r
r d t u r j k s a l s
s s y i f i r t s a t
t f i r s t u i t e f
b n l m p l o u e v a
s a f i r s t w a t s
f s t s r n f i r s t
f a s t d w u y i l b
```

48

Sight Words: gave & goes

Circle the socks with **gave**.

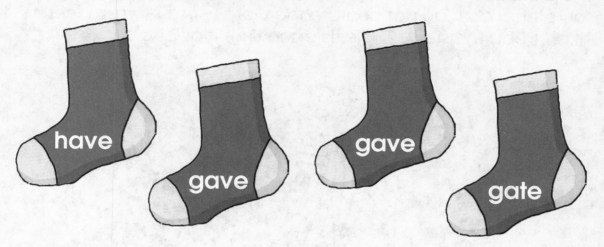

Circle the socks with **goes**.

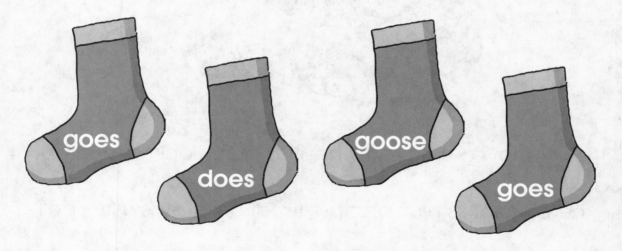

Circle **gave** or **goes** in each sentence.

That sock goes in this drawer.

My mom gave me money for doing chores.

Sight Word: its

The word **its** is a possessive. It shows that something is owned by something else. Do not confuse the word with **it's**, which means "it is." Read the story. Circle **its** each time it appears.

I know a cute cat who lives at the animal shelter.

The color of its fur is orange. Its favorite toy is a big ball

of string. Its favorite place to sit is on the windowsill. Its

favorite activity is pouncing on people's shoelaces!

When it's time for treats, the cat meows loudly. Then,

it's time for a long nap on its blanket.

Sight Words: made & many

Color the boxes with **made** pink. Color the boxes with **many** yellow.

many	mane	any	made
made	many	make	mad
male	mud	made	mole
made	mean	man	zany
may	many	fade	made
many	mad	many	man

51

Sight Words: off & or

Write **off** or **or** to complete each sentence.

We could stay home, _____ we could go
to the soccer game.

The wind blew the leaves _____ the trees.

Would you rather build a snowman _____
go sledding?

My umbrella kept the rain _____ my head.

Write **pull** or **read** to complete each sentence.

Donna must _____ the weeds before she plants flowers.

Mrs. Higgins and Adam _____ to the class.

Juan uses the wagon to _____ his toys.

Ryder found a book to _____ on the trip.

Sight Words: right & sing

Circle the balloons with **right**.

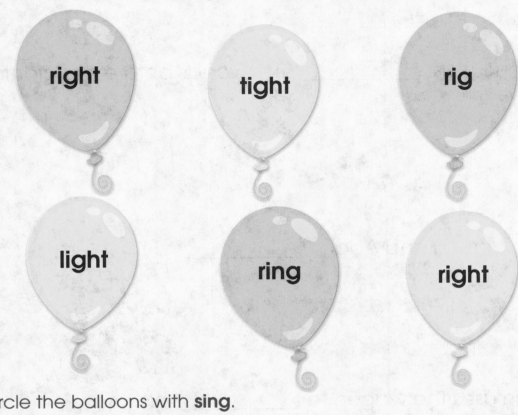

Circle the balloons with **sing**.

Sight Words: tell & their

The word **their** is used to show that something is owned. Do not confuse it with **there**, which names a place, or with **they're**, which means "they are." Circle **their** in each sentence.

The students went over there to sharpen their pencils.

They're bringing their famous chili to the party.

Circle **tell** in each box.

sell tilt tell

tell bell let

Call 9-1-1 only in a real emergency. Call if someone is seriously injured, if you see signs of fire, or if someone is in danger. When you call, be ready to **tell**:

9-1-1

- What the emergency is.

- Where you are. (If you don't know the address, tell what roads or places are nearby.)

- What phone number you are calling from.

- Who is hurt or in need of rescue.

Health & Fitness

Sight Words: these & those

Underline **these** and **those** in the sentences.

What will grow from these seeds?

Are these rain boots yours?

Those boys are cheering loudly.

Those flowers smell so good!

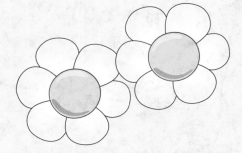

I saw those cookies at the store, but I like these better.

I washed all of these dishes, but those will have to wait.

Sight Words: upon & us

Find and circle **upon** and **us** in the puzzle. Each word appears six times. Look across and down. Circle **upon** in **red**. Circle **us** in orange.

```
p  t  r  i  o  s  u  s  n  m  b  c
i  o  f  e  s  a  i  k  l  u  s  p
e  u  p  o  n  r  o  b  n  p  i  s
a  s  e  r  t  c  u  e  t  o  v  p
e  t  r  n  m  g  p  c  t  n  d  f
t  o  l  e  c  r  o  b  e  b  r  l
y  u  b  u  p  o  n  i  l  v  y  u
u  w  p  u  d  x  z  w  q  y  k  e
p  e  o  s  e  h  f  h  j  u  t  h
o  b  u  d  v  t  u  p  o  n  r  e
n  m  y  e  r  w  u  n  o  s  u  s
x  u  s  k  l  h  r  c  e  w  r  j
```

Sight Words: use & very

Write the missing letters to spell **use**.

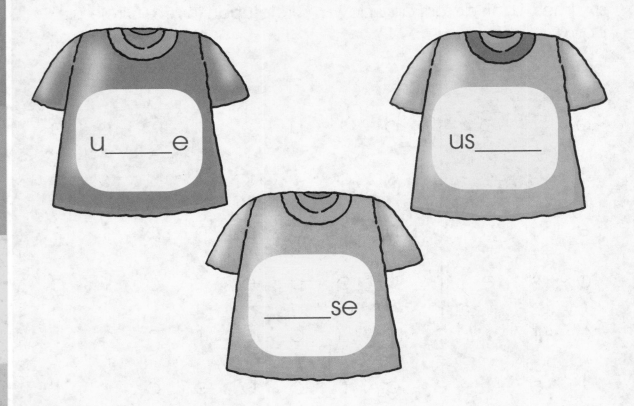

u_____e

us_____

_____se

Circle **very** in each sentence.

It would take a very long time to travel around the world.

The snow kept falling, so we made a very tall snowman!

Don't touch! The boiling water is very hot.

Sight Words: which & why

Circle **which** or **why** to complete each sentence.

_____ do you prefer, the green shirt or the purple one?

Which **Why**

_____ did you choose to play baseball?

Which **Why**

_____ is Mrs. Posy wearing a bandage?

Which **Why**

I don't know _____ way to go.

which **why**

What do you dream of doing someday? Complete the title. Then, write to explain **why** you want to make your dream come true.

Why I Want to _____

_____

_____

_____

_____

Sight Words: work & write

Color the boxes with **work** green. Color the boxes with **write** orange.

work	worm	write	while
write	word	awhile	twine
whirl	write	wring	write
white	whale	work	wrong
work	write	worry	warm
why	work	wore	work

Sight Words: Would & your

Read the puppet play. Circle **would** each time you see it.
Underline **your** each time you see it.

Pip: Would you like to hear a joke?

Pep: Sure! Tell me your best one.

Pip: What kind of burger would a polar bear eat?

Pep: I don't know. Your riddle has stumped me!

Pip: I knew you would never guess. It's an iceberg-er!

Pep: Good one! Would you like to hear my joke now?

Pip: Would I ever!

Pep: Why is your math book sad?

Pip: I'm not sure. Your joke is a tough one.

Pep: Your math book is sad because it has so
         many problems!

Circle what you **would** do in each situation.

If I had a group project at school, I would

      let others do the work.   **do my fair share.**

If I heard kids saying mean things about a classmate, I would

      tell them to stop.   **join in.**

If my parent was sick, I would

      do whatever I wanted.   **offer to help with chores.**

Context Clues

Complete the story with words from the box. Use context clues to help you.

> roasting   nodded   enormous   cheerful
> disappointed   lengthy   quickly

On Saturday, Dad and I went to the dog park. It was a cold day, but I was _____ by the time we walked all the way there. The park was filled with all kinds of dogs. There were tiny dogs with short fur and _____ dogs with _____ fur. They were running and jumping all around. I have never seen such a _____ group of dogs! I knew I would feel _____ when it was time to leave.

A small mutt came up to me. I threw a ball, and he _____ ran to fetch it.

"Dad," I said, "we need a dog of our own."

Dad _____. "That's just what I was thinking."

Context Clues

Complete the story with words from the box. Use context clues to help you.

> fluffy   sample   savory   gobble
> raw   nibbled   bare

One sunny day, my whole family had a picnic at the park. My grandmother prepared _____ chicken. Grandpa baked some _____ rolls. My uncle brought _____ vegetables and dip. My mom made something green and white in a big dish. I ate the chicken, two rolls, and some vegetables. I liked it all! Then, my brother looked in the dish our mom had brought.

"Did you try it?" I asked him.

"You're my big brother, " he said. "You _____ it!"

I _____ a tiny bit. It was good! But the dish was almost _____. "It's terrible!" I told my brother. "I'll eat the rest of it so you won't have to."

My brother watched me _____ it all up. I tried not to look too happy!

Classifying

Write a word from the box to tell what could be described by each group of words.

soup	puppy	storm	ocean	book
dishes	winter		kite	car

sand
shells
waves
fish
_____

snow
wind
cold
ice
_____

string
tail
wind
fly
_____

rain
thunder
wind
hail
_____

soft
furry
playful
small
_____

broth
carrots
tomatoes
noodles
_____

cup
plate
bowl
platter
_____

pages
words
pictures
cover
_____

tires
seats
window
trunk
_____

Classifying

Draw an **X** on the word in each row that does not belong.

| apple pie | peas | pudding | ice cream |

| green beans | cucumbers | corn | bread |

| peaches | oranges | chicken | apples |

| cheese | milk | rice | yogurt |

| napkin | spoon | salad | knife |

Healthy snacks provide energy to help you work, play, and learn. Look at the **classified** healthy snacks. Write one more in each category.

Fruits	**Vegetables**
apple	celery sticks
raisins	cherry tomatoes
_____	_____

Grains	**Dairy**
granola bar	cheese stick
wheat crackers	chocolate milk
_____	_____

Prefixes

Change the meaning of each sentence by adding the prefix to the **bold** word.

The girl felt **lucky** because she answered the questions **correctly**.

The girl felt (un) _____ because she

answered the questions (in) _____.

When Jayden **behaved**, he felt **happy**.

When Jayden (mis) _____, he

felt (un) _____.

Bryce wanted to **paint** the picture because he **liked** it.

Bryce wanted to (re) _____ the picture

because he (dis) _____ it.

Suffixes

Add the suffixes to the base words. Write the new words and use them to complete the sentences below.

help + ing = _____   talk + ed = _____

care + less = _____   love + ly = _____

build + er = _____   loud + er = _____

My mother _____ to my teacher about the field trip.

The radio was _____ than the television.

Those flowers are _____!

Madison was being _____ when she lost the permission slip.

Marshall thinks he is the best _____ when it comes to blocks.

Kyle is _____ to fold the laundry.

Base Words

Look at the first word in each row. Circle its base word.

starring	star	starred
looking	looked	look
recycle	cycle	cycling
preview	view	viewing
unfriendly	friendly	friend
happier	unhappy	happy

Underline the **base word** shared by each pair of words. Then, circle the word in each pair that best describes you.

helpful	disrespectful	friendly	flexible
unhelpful	respectful	unfriendly	inflexible

Word Parts

Look at each word. Write its prefix, base word, and suffix in the chart. Not all words have all three parts. You may need to change the spelling of the base word. The first one is done for you.

	Prefix	Base Word	Suffix
tallest		tall	est
unhappy			
recycling			
unfairly			
informal			
distrusted			
thankful			
underground			
younger			
misspoke			
rewritten			
incorrectly			

Shades of Meaning

Look at each group of words. Which word has the strongest meaning? Use it to complete the sentence.

fell   **crashed**   **tumbled**

The glass plate _____ to the ground.

plunges   **hops**   **leaps**

The frog _____ into the pond.

devoured   **ate**   **nibbled**

The boy quickly _____ his breakfast.

Write a stronger word for the **bold** word in each sentence.

"Hello, Mrs. Carter," Hannah **said**.   _____

The children **walk** out the door
when the bell rings.   _____

Ahmed and I really **like** this movie.   _____

Shades of Meaning

Look at each group of words. Which word has the strongest meaning? Use it to complete the sentence.

angry   **cross**   **furious**

Tonio was _____ with his brother.

tasty   **delicious**   **yummy**

My dad cooked a _____ dinner tonight.

pretty   **nice**   **stunning**

The flowers in your garden are _____!

Write a stronger word for the **bold** word in each sentence.

The **hungry** cat sat near its
empty bowl.   _____

Playing basketball is **fun**.   _____

The movie we watched last night
was **bad**.   _____

Compound Words

Compound words are two smaller words that are put together to make one new word. Match words in each column to make compound words. Write the words on the lines. The first one is done for you.

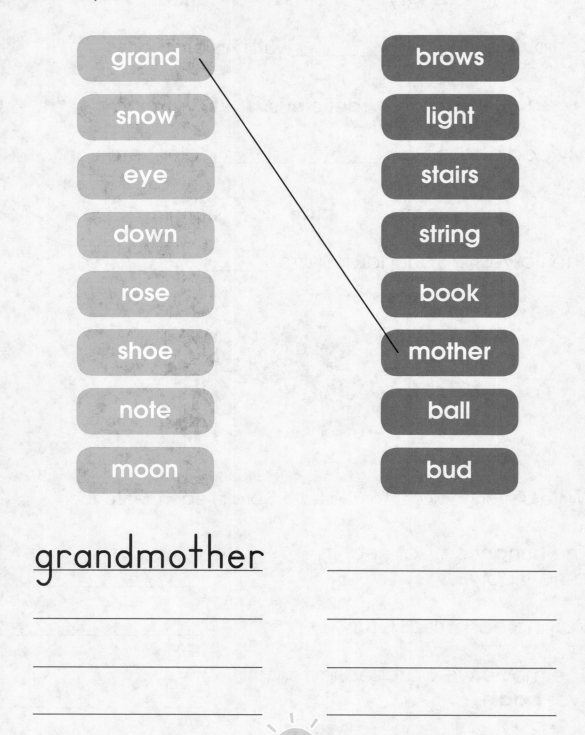

grand	brows
snow	light
eye	stairs
down	string
rose	book
shoe	mother
note	ball
moon	bud

grandmother

_____   _____

_____   _____

_____   _____

Compound Words

Combine two words from the box to make a compound word that names each picture. You may use the words more than once.

box	room	hall	rain	sand	melon
way	bed	water	lunch	coat	

_____   _____

_____   _____

_____   _____

Playing a sport is a good way to stay fit and healthy. Combine each word with **ball** to make a **compound word** that names a sport. Circle your favorite sport to play.

volley_____   foot_____

kick_____   basket_____

base_____   soft_____

Compound Words

Read each compound word. Write the two smaller words that make it up. How do the meanings of the smaller words relate to the meaning of each compound word?

pigpen

_____

_____

beehive

_____

_____

broomstick

_____

_____

starfish

_____

_____

sidewalk

_____

_____

sunburn

_____

_____

campfire

_____

_____

outdoors

_____

_____

cardboard

_____

_____

Compound Words

Combine the underlined words to make a compound word that answers each question.

What is a <u>berry</u> that is <u>blue</u>? _____

What is the <u>time</u> to go to <u>bed</u>? _____

What is a <u>room</u> for a <u>class</u>? _____

What is the <u>top</u> of a <u>tree</u>? _____

What is a <u>case</u> for a <u>book</u>? _____

What is a <u>place</u> for a <u>fire</u>? _____

What is a <u>pan</u> for a <u>dish</u>? _____

What is a <u>cloth</u> for the <u>table</u>? _____

Dictionary Skills

The words in a dictionary are arranged in alphabetical order. Look at each group of words. Circle the word that comes first in alphabetical order. If two words begin with the same letter, look at their second letters, third letters, and so on.

duck

four

rock

chair

carry

yellow

peach

this

walk

rope

look

luck

light

come

one

mouse

mouth

music

foot

boat

mine

who

whole

wonder

angel

able

hair

Dictionary Skills

The guide words at the top of a dictionary page tell what the first and last words on that page will be. Only words that come in alphabetical order between those two words will be on that page. Write each word in alphabetical order between the guide words.

| faint | fan | fence | farm | feed |
| family | farmer | face | far | feet |

face   **fence**

_____   _____

_____   _____

_____   _____

_____   _____

_____   _____

Dictionary Skills

A picture dictionary contains words, word meanings, and pictures. Complete the picture dictionary page. Write the missing definitions.

baby

_____

band

a group of people that plays music

bank

a place where money is kept

bark

_____

berry

_____

board

a flat piece of wood

Dictionary Skills

When words have more than one meaning, the meanings are numbered in a dictionary. Read the meanings for **tag**. Write the number of the correct definition after each sentence.

tag

1. a small strip or tab attached to something else
2. to label
3. to follow closely and constantly
4. a game of chase

We will play a game of **tag** after we eat. _____

My little sister will **tag** along with us. _____

The **tag** on my shirt shows the size. _____

The scientist will **tag** the duck and track it. _____

Read the **dictionary** entry. Then, write about whether each meaning of the word describes you.

patient *adjective* 1. Able to handle trouble or delay without complaining. 2. Not hasty or in a hurry to finish.

_____

_____

_____

_____

Nouns

Decide whether each noun names a person, place, or thing. Write it under the correct category. Then, circle each common noun. Draw a box around each proper noun.

> bridge   Elm Park   Malik Jones   cousin
> park   Golden Gate Bridge

Person

_____

Place

_____

Thing

_____

Look at each **common noun**. Write a matching **proper noun** that names someone who is special to you. Draw a picture of each person.

teacher	relative	friend

_____   _____   _____

Collective Nouns

A collective noun names a group of people, animals, or things. Circle the collective noun in each phrase. Then, match it to the group it names.

a school of

a class of

a swarm of

a bunch of

a pride of

Plurals

Write the plural of each noun. Add **s** or **es**. If the word ends in **y**, change **y** to **i** before adding **es**. If the word ends in **f** or **fe**, change **f** to **v** before adding **s** or **es**.

dog   penny

_____   _____

ax   class

_____   _____

peach   blueberry

_____   _____

party   wife

_____   _____

boot   city

_____   _____

leaf   walrus

_____   _____

Irregular Plurals

The plurals of some nouns do not follow the rules you know. Look at the noun above each sentence. Write its irregular plural to finish the sentence.

feet   teeth   deer   children   women

tooth

I lost my two front _____.

woman

The _____ in Mom's club are best friends.

foot

The clown had big _____.

child

The _____ played hide-and-seek.

deer

_____ live in this forest.

Pronouns

Rewrite each sentence using a pronoun to replace the noun in **bold**.

| her | them | they | he | it |

The owl has a nest in the old barn.

_____

Give the books to **Ethan and Tara**.

_____

Marcus watched the bird land.

_____

Everyone cheered for **Alice**.

_____

Georgia and Finn went to the zoo.

_____

Reflexive Pronouns

Reflexive pronouns refer back to a noun in the sentence. They often end in **-self** or **-selves**. Write a reflexive pronoun to complete each sentence.

> **myself**   **ourselves**   **herself**   **itself**
> **himself**   **yourselves**

My little sister likes to dress _____.

"Behave _____," said the teacher to her students.

I taught _____ how to roller skate.

My brother drove _____ to school today.

We entertained _____ by playing with cars.

Maya's dog ran away, but it came back home

by _____.

Verbs

Underline the verb in each sentence about spiders. The verb tells what spiders do or what spiders are.

A spider is an arachnid.

Spiders spin webs of silk.

They wait in the center of their webs.

Then, they sink their fangs into trapped insects.

Female spiders wrap silk around their eggs for protection.

Most spiders are harmless to people.

Do spiders scare you?

Write a **verb** to complete each sentence.

I can _____.

I can _____.

I can't _____ yet, but
I will keep trying and getting better!

Verb Tenses

Write **past**, **present**, or **future** to tell the tense of the verb in each sentence.

It will rain tomorrow. _____

Tomas is singing a song. _____

He played lacrosse. _____

I will buy a sandwich. _____

Molly is sleeping. _____

Dad worked hard today. _____

Find the verb in each sentence. Rewrite it in the tense shown.

Mia played with her new friend. (present) _____

Hasaan is calling him. (future) _____

Holly and Luisa walk here. (past) _____

Irregular Verbs

Some past-tense verbs do not follow the rules you know. They do not end in **ed**. Rewrite each sentence in the past tense. Use an irregular verb.

| blew | gave | grew | took | came |

I will grow another inch this year.

_____

I will blow out the candles.

_____

Everyone will give me presents.

_____

All my cousins will come.

_____

The party will take three hours.

_____

Irregular Verbs

Circle the irregular verb that completes each sentence.

Scientists have (find, found) the cure.

The coach (speaks, spoke) to us yesterday.

The teacher (rings, rang) the bell earlier.

She (says, said) it twice already.

Grace (sings, sang) in the school concert last year.

89

Irregular Verbs

Write verbs to complete the chart.

Present Tense	Past Tense	Future Tense
It _____	It went	It will go
She has	She _____	She will have
He _____	He saw	He will see
It eats	It ate	It _____
She leaves	She _____	She will leave
He makes	He made	He _____
It flies	It _____	It will fly
She _____	She wore	She will wear

Irregular Verbs

Use past-tense verbs from the chart on page 90 to complete the sentences.

The plane _____ high above the clouds.

We _____ cranberries for Thanksgiving last year.

Cinnamon _____ that bread taste so good.

Last weekend, we _____ camping in our favorite spot by the lake.

Grandpa already _____ to go to the store.

We _____ a great time at the party.

My sister _____ a dragon costume for Halloween.

She _____ a raccoon under the bridge.

91

Irregular Verbs

The verb **be** is different from all other verbs. The present-tense forms of **be** are **am**, **is**, and **are**. Write **am**, **is**, or **are** to complete each sentence.

My friends _____ helping me build a tree house.

It _____ in my backyard.

We _____ using hammers, wood, and nails.

It _____ a very hard job.

I _____ lucky to have such good friends.

Irregular Verbs

The verb **be** is different from all other verbs. The past-tense forms of **be** are **was** and **were**. Circle **was** or **were** to complete each sentence.

I _____ outside raking leaves.   **was**   **were**

Raindrops _____ starting to fall.   **was**   **were**

Soon, it _____ pouring.   **was**   **were**

The leaves _____ getting soaked.   **was**   **were**

It _____ time to go inside!   **was**   **were**

Adjectives

Adjectives describe nouns. They answer questions like these: What kind? How many? How much? Write two adjectives from the story that describe each **bold** noun.

Super Soup

On a cold winter **morning**, my mom said, "Let's make soup. It will be ready for lunch." We made a pot of hot vegetable **soup**. First, I put sweet white **onions** in the pot. Then, I added three cleaned **carrots**. Next into the pot were ripe, juicy **tomatoes**. Last, we added crisp, fresh **potatoes**. The soup cooked for a long time. Finally, we ate our super soup for lunch as snowflakes swirled outside. It was the best soup I ever had!

morning	onions	carrots
_____	_____	_____
_____	_____	_____

tomatoes	potatoes	soup
_____	_____	_____
_____	_____	_____

Read **adjectives** from **a** to **z**. Circle those that describe you!

adventurous	**f**riendly	**m**essy	**t**alented
brave	**g**enerous	**n**eat	**u**nderstanding
curious	**h**elpful	**o**ptimistic	**v**ocal
daring	**i**nventive	**p**atient	**w**atchful
energetic	**j**olly	**q**uiet	e**x**traordinary
	kind	**r**eliable	**y**oung
	loyal	**s**mart	**z**any

All About Me

Adverbs

Adverbs describe verbs. They often end in **ly**. They answer questions like these: Where? How? When? Circle the adverb in each sentence. Write the adverb to answer the question.

The doctor listened carefully.

How did the doctor listen? _____

The call was returned yesterday.

When was the call returned? _____

She lost her shoes somewhere.

Where did she lose her shoes? _____

He did the work perfectly.

How did he do the work? _____

They often jump rope.

When do they jump rope? _____

Adjectives & Adverbs

Circle the adjective or adverb that describes the **bold** word and completes the sentence.

The sun **rose** _____ in the East.

quick   quickly

Vera kicked the _____ **ball** into the air.

bouncy   bouncily

Paul _____ **peeked** around the corner.

slow   slowly

Corey did not study and got a _____ **grade**.

bad   badly

Sari's _____ **project** won first prize.

creative   creatively

I **thought** _____ before I made my next move.

serious   seriously

Adjectives & Adverbs

Circle the adjective or adverb that completes each sentence. If you circle an adjective, underline the noun it describes. If you circle an adverb, underline the verb it describes.

The cat (**quiet, quietly**) slept under the table.

The (**brave, bravely**) police officer helped the boy.

The couple danced to the (**loud, loudly**) song.

My little brother (**neat, neatly**) made his bed.

Underline an **adjective** or an **adverb** in each bike safety rule.

Wear a snug helmet.

Ride near a buddy.

Dress in bright colors.

Check to see if the brakes work well.

Do not ride in dim light.

Inflate tires fully.

97

Expand Sentences

Use the adjectives and adverbs shown to expand and rewrite each sentence.

swiftly   **old**

Parker ran down the dirt path.

_____

_____

loyal   **dearly**

Seth loves his dog.

_____

_____

always   **pink**

Ana wears glasses.

_____

_____

colorful   **everywhere**

Before the party, Mom hung banners.

_____

_____

Expand Sentences

Add adjectives, adverbs, and other words to expand the
sentences and provide more information.

The friends chatted.

_____

_____

Their team lost the game.

_____

_____

Squirrels chased each other.

_____

_____

His phone buzzed.

_____

_____

The storm raged.

_____

_____

Simple Sentences

A simple sentence has one noun/verb pair. The noun part of the sentence is the subject. The verb part of the sentence is the predicate. Circle the noun in each simple sentence. Underline the verb in each simple sentence. Draw a line between the subject and the predicate. The first one is done for you.

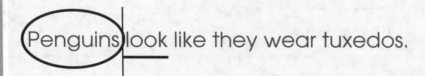 

(Penguins) | look like they wear tuxedos.

Monkeys swing on bars.

Harbor seals eat raw fish.

Bats roost in cool, dark places.

The peacock has brilliant feathers.

Giraffes' long necks stretch into treetops.

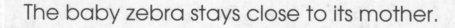

The baby zebra stays close to its mother.

Simple Sentences

When the subject (noun part) of a sentence has two nouns, it is a compound subject. When the predicate (verb part) of a sentence has two verbs, it is a compound predicate. Combine each pair of sentences into one simple sentence with a compound subject, compound predicate, or both. You will need to add the word **and**. The first one is done for you.

The gymnast grabbed the bar. The gymnast flipped.

The gymnast grabbed the bar and flipped.

Roses grow in the garden. Tulips grow in the garden.

_____

_____

Dad chopped firewood. Dad stacked firewood.

_____

_____

Coats keep us warm in winter. Sweaters keep us warm in winter.

_____

_____

Students choose books. Students read silently.

_____

_____

Compound Sentences

A compound sentence has two noun/verb pairs or two subjects and two predicates. Each subject/predicate pair could stand alone as a simple sentence. The two parts are joined by one of these conjunctions: **for**, **and**, **nor**, **but**, **or**, **yet**, **so**. Combine each pair of simple sentences into one compound sentence. Use the conjunction shown. The first one is done for you.

and   I have a dog. Shawnda has a cat.

<u>I have a dog, and Shawnda has</u>
<u>a cat.</u>

but   The sun is shining. The air is cold.

_____

_____

or   Would you rather eat at home? Would you rather go out?

_____

_____

so   We made our presentation into a game show. Everyone paid attention.

_____

_____

Compound Sentences

Write compound sentences. Choose one subject/predicate pair from the first box, a conjunction from the middle box, and one subject/predicate pair from the last box.

Libby could go to the festival,

Libby went to the festival,

Libby rode the roller coaster,

Libby played arcade games,

and
but
or

she rode the Ferris wheel.

she did not win any prizes.

she could stay home.

she did not stay long.

1. _____

   _____

2. _____

   _____

3. _____

   _____

4. _____

   _____

Capitalization

Names of places on the map, names of holidays, and brand names begin with a capital letter. Write the words where they belong. Begin each important word with a capital letter. One is done for you.

north america	earth day	niagara falls
high jump shoes	memorial day	write brite crayons

Brand Names

High Jump shoes _____

Places on the Map

_____ _____

Holidays

_____ _____

Draw a picture of your favorite place on the map, holiday, and product. Write their names. Begin each important word with a **capital** letter.

Place: _____ Holiday: _____ Product: _____

_____ _____ _____

All About Me

Commas

Follow the directions to write a letter to a family member or friend.

_____

Write the month, the day, a comma (,), and the year.

_____

Write a greeting that begins with **Dear**. Then, write the person's name. Write a comma (,) after the person's name.

_____

Write a friendly message.

_____

_____

_____

_____

_____

Write a closing. Some closings are: **Sincerely**, **Yours Truly**, or **Your Friend**. Write a comma (,) after the closing.

_____

Sign your name on the line below the closing.

Contractions

A contraction joins two words into one. An apostrophe (') takes the place of the missing letters. When we speak, we often use contractions. For example, we say **don't** instead of **do not**. Draw a line from each word pair to its contraction.

I am	you're
you are	we'll
we will	I'm

they are	he'd
are not	they're
he would	aren't

Underline two words in each sentence that could make a contraction. Write the contraction.

He is not afraid of heights. _____

I would like some soup, please. _____

Is not that a pretty bird? _____

Contractions

Write the two words that make up each contraction.

we've _____ + _____   I'm _____ + _____

she's _____ + _____   you'll _____ + _____

can't _____ + _____   haven't _____ + _____

Write the words as contractions.

you have _____   I am _____

they are _____   he will _____

it will _____   they had _____

had not _____   is not _____

Having a growth mindset means believing that hard work will help you learn, grow, and reach your goals. Look at the chart to see how to change limiting thoughts into thoughts that show a growth mindset. Circle a **contraction** in each sentence.

Instead of…	Try thinking…
I'm not good at this.	I'm going to keep getting better.
I'd better just give up.	I'll try a different way.
I'll never be that smart.	I'm getting smarter all the time.

Possessives

To show ownership, add an apostrophe (') and **s** after the noun. For singular nouns, write the apostrophe before **s**. For plural nouns, write the apostrophe after **s**. A snack owned by one girl is the girl's snack. A snack owned by two girls is the girls' snack. Look at each **bold** word. Write the correct possessive noun.

The **lions** cage was big enough for all of them. _____

The **bears** costumes were purple. _____

One **boys** laughter was very loud. _____

Marks cotton candy was delicious. _____

Lauras sister clapped for the clowns. _____

Possessives

Circle the correct possessive noun for each sentence.

One _____ mother is a teacher.

girl's   **girls'**

The _____ tail is long.

cat's   **cats'**

The _____ aprons are white.

server's   **servers'**

These _____ collars are different colors.

dog's   **dogs'**

My five _____ uniforms are dirty.

brother's   **brothers'**

The _____ doll is cute.

child's   **childs'**

Apostrophes

Read each word. Notice how the apostrophe is used. If the word is a contraction, circle **C**. If the word is a possessive noun, circle **P**.

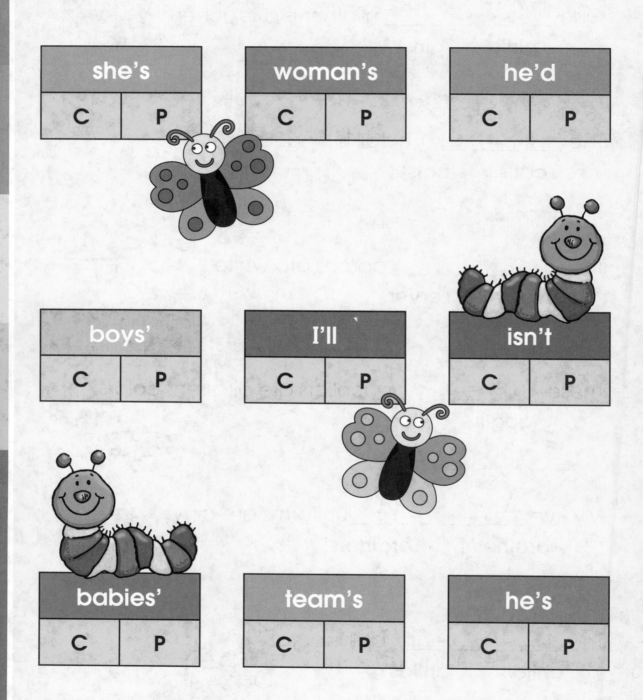

she's		woman's		he'd	
C	P	C	P	C	P

boys'		I'll		isn't	
C	P	C	P	C	P

babies'		team's		he's	
C	P	C	P	C	P

Apostrophes

Circle the contractions and possessive nouns that are written correctly. Write the other words correctly under the category where they belong.

mans'	Il'l	wouldve'
weren't	we'll	sh'es
ca'nt	Victor's	I've
baby's	womans'	wolfs'
childs'	you're	wolves'

Contractions

_____

_____

_____

_____

Possessives

_____

_____

_____

_____

111

Sequence

Read about rain. Then, follow the instructions.

Clouds are made of little drops of ice and water. The drops push and bang into each other. Then, they join together to make bigger drops and begin to fall. More raindrops cling to them. They become heavy and fall quickly to the ground.

Write **first**, **second**, **third**, **fourth**, and **fifth** to put the events in order.

_____ More raindrops cling to them.

_____ Clouds are made of little drops of ice and water.

_____ They join together and make bigger drops that begin to fall.

_____ The drops of ice and water bang into each other.

_____ The drops become heavy and fall quickly to the ground.

Read things you might say to make a new friend. **Sequence** them by writing **first**, **second**, **third**, and **fourth**.

Social Skills

_____ It is nice to meet you.

_____ What game do you want to play?

_____ Hi, my name is…

_____ Would you like to play a game?

Sequence

Read the story. Then, follow the instructions.

One Saturday morning in May, Olivia and Anna went to the zoo. First, they bought tickets to get into the zoo. Second, they visited the Gorilla Garden and had fun watching the gorillas stare at them. Then, they went to Tiger Town and watched the tigers as they slept in the sunshine. Fourth, they went to Hippo Haven and laughed at the hippos cooling off in their pool. Next, the girls visited Snake Station and learned about poisonous and nonpoisonous snakes. It was noon, and they were hungry, so they ate lunch at Parrot Patio.

Write **first**, **second**, **third**, **fourth**, **fifth**, and **sixth** to put the events in order.

_____ They went to Hippo Haven.

_____ Olivia and Anna bought zoo tickets.

_____ They watched the tigers sleep.

_____ They ate lunch at Parrot Patio.

_____ The gorillas stared at them.

_____ They learned about snakes.

Classify

Use a **red** crayon to circle the names of three animals that would make good pets. Use a **blue** crayon to circle the names of three wild animals. Use an **orange** crayon to circle the two animals that live on a farm.

bear	lion	bird	cow
cat	sheep	dog	tiger

```
a m e o w w n l i o n
b m d o g g x i i s o
a b e a r r v l m h r
r m r m o o u s e e k
k c a b b i r d s e m
i o t t i g e r m p q
b w n o w r q n e n
d n c p h h i d u d n
f k c a t t r o a r m
```

Classify

Write words from the box where they belong.

bush	strawberries	apple juice
airplane	honey	grass
rocket	flower	bird

These things taste sweet.

_____ _____ _____

These things can fly.

_____ _____ _____

These things grow in the ground.

_____ _____ _____

People with a growth mindset believe that, through hard work, they can change, grow, and learn. **Classify** the thoughts. Draw a line from each one to **Fixed Mindset** or **Growth Mindset**.

Growth Mindset

I can either do it, or I can't.

There is no limit to how much I can learn.

I stick to what I know.

Challenges help me grow.

Fixed Mindset

Compare & Contrast

Read about Emma and Lee. Then, write how they are the same and different in the Venn diagram.

Emma and Lee like to play ball. They like to jump rope. Lee likes to play a card game called "Old Maid." Emma likes to play a card game called "Go Fish." What do you do to have fun?

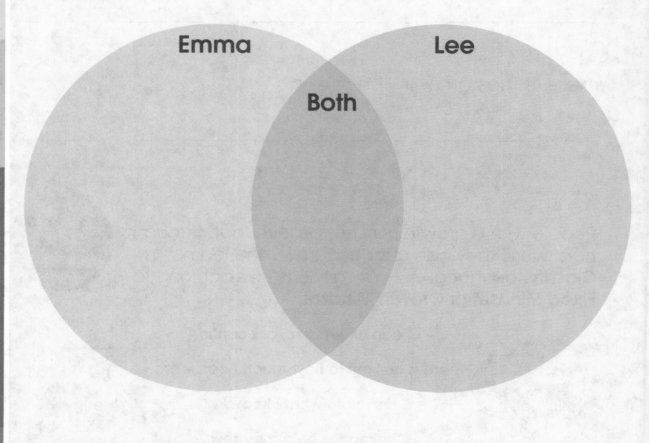

Emma

Lee

Both

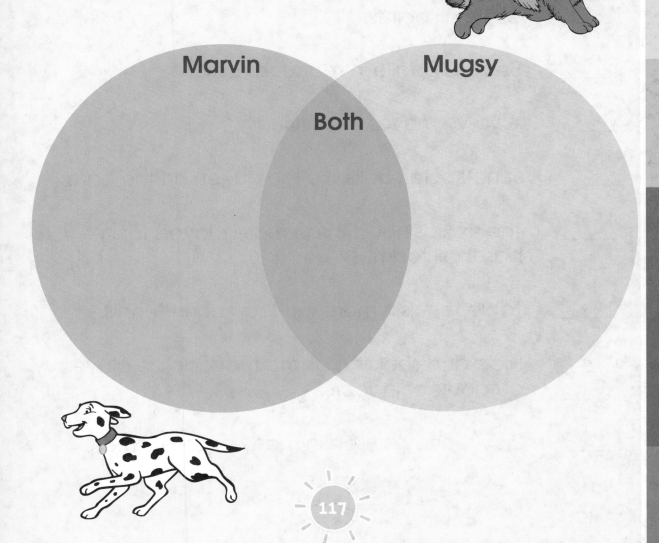

Compare & Contrast

Read about Marvin and Mugsy. Then, complete the Venn diagram, telling how they are the same and different.

Maggie has two dogs, Marvin and Mugsy. Marvin is a dalmatian. Marvin likes to run after balls in the backyard. His favorite food is Canine Crunchy Crunch. Maggie likes to take Marvin for walks. Then, Marvin loves to sleep in his doghouse. Mugsy is a big, furry brown dog. Since she is big, she needs lots of exercise. Maggie takes her for walks in the park. Her favorite food is Canine Crunchy Crunch. Mugsy likes to sleep on Maggie's bed.

Marvin   **Mugsy**

Both

Fact & Opinion

A fact can be proven. An opinion is a feeling or belief that cannot be proven. Write **F** next to each fact and **O** next to each opinion.

_____ Tennis is cool!

_____ There are red and black markers in a checkers game.

_____ In football, a touchdown is worth six points.

_____ Being a goalie in soccer is easy.

_____ A yo-yo moves on a string.

_____ June's sister looks like the queen on the card.

_____ The six kids need three more players for a baseball team.

_____ Table tennis is more fun than court tennis.

_____ Hide-and-seek is a game that can be played outdoors or indoors.

_____ Play money is used in many board games.

Fact & Opinion

Read the story. Write **F** next to each fact and **O** next to each opinion.

My name is Henrietta, and I am a humpback whale. I live in cold seas in the summer and warm seas in the winter. My long flippers are used to move forward and backward. I like to eat fish. Sometimes, I show off by leaping out of the water. Would you like to be a humpback whale?

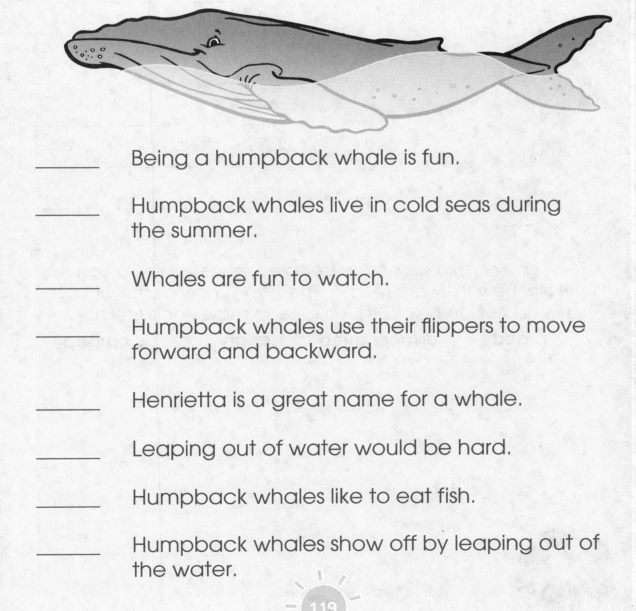

_____ Being a humpback whale is fun.

_____ Humpback whales live in cold seas during the summer.

_____ Whales are fun to watch.

_____ Humpback whales use their flippers to move forward and backward.

_____ Henrietta is a great name for a whale.

_____ Leaping out of water would be hard.

_____ Humpback whales like to eat fish.

_____ Humpback whales show off by leaping out of the water.

Predict

Look at each picture. Draw and write what you predict will happen next.

_____

_____

_____

_____

_____

_____

_____

_____

Recognizing expressions on people's faces can help you **predict** how they are feeling. Then, you know better what to say and how to help. Draw a face to show each feeling.

proud	disappointed	angry	surprised

Predict

Read the story. Then, answer the questions.

Maggie had a great idea for a game to play with her dogs Marvin and Mugsy. The game was called "Dog Derby." Maggie would stand at one end of the driveway and hold on to the dogs by their collars. Her friend Mitch would stand at the other end of the driveway. When he said, "Go!" Maggie would let go of the dogs and they would race to Mitch. The first one there would get a dog biscuit. If there was a tie, both dogs would get a biscuit.

Which dog do you think will win the race?

_____

Why? _____

_____

What do you think will happen when they race again?

_____

_____

Answer Questions

Read about snakes. Then, answer the questions.

There are many facts about snakes that might surprise people. A snake's skin is dry. Most snakes are shy. They will hide from people. Snakes eat mice and rats. They do not chew them up. Snakes' jaws drop open so they can swallow their food whole.

A snake's skin is _____.

Most snakes are _____.

Snakes eat _____ and _____.

How do snakes eat? _____

_____

Did any facts about snakes surprise you? Which ones?

_____

_____

Answer Questions

Read about sharks. Then, answer the questions.

Angela learned a lot about sharks when her class visited the aquarium. She learned that sharks are fish. Some sharks are as big as an elephant, and some can fit into a small paper bag. Sharks have no bones. They have hundreds of teeth, and when they lose them, they grow new ones. They eat animals of any kind. Whale sharks are the largest of all fish.

Some sharks are as big as _____.

Sharks have _____ of teeth.

_____ are the largest of all fish.

Sharks are fish. True or false? _____

Do sharks have bones? _____

Write a Story

Complete the sentences to write a story about a school trip.

The second-graders went on a trip to _____

_____.

The bus ride there was _____

_____.

When they arrived, they _____

_____.

Next, they _____

_____.

Finally, the class _____

_____.

The field trip was _____

_____.

Write a Story

Write a story about the picture. Describe the characters, setting, and events. Remember to include a beginning, a middle, and an ending.

_____

_____

_____

_____

_____

_____

_____

_____

_____

_____

_____

Write a Story

Plan a story about the picture. Complete the graphic organizer.

Characters

Description:

_____

_____

_____

Description:

_____

_____

_____

Description:

_____

_____

_____

Setting

The story takes place

_____

_____.

This place:

looks _____.

sounds _____.

smells _____.

Events

The main problem in the story is _____

_____.

The first thing that happens is _____.

The next thing that happens is _____.

The last thing that happens is _____.

The solution to the problem is _____

_____.

126

Write a Story

Use the planner you made on page 126. Write your story below.

_____

_____

_____

_____

_____

_____

_____

_____

_____

_____

_____

_____

Write to Inform

How do you make a mug of hot chocolate with marshmallows? Complete the sentences to write step-by-step directions.

Hot chocolate is _____

_____.

The first step for making hot chocolate is _____

_____.

The next step is _____

_____.

The last step for making hot chocolate is _____

_____.

Enjoy your hot chocolate! Do not forget to _____

_____.

Write to Inform

Can you explain how to ride a bicycle? Write step-by-step directions.

Riding a bicycle is _____

_____ .

First, you _____

_____ .

Then, you _____

_____ .

Last, you _____

_____ .

With some practice, you will find that riding a bike is ____

_____ .

Write to Inform

With an adult, do some research to learn facts about the city or state where you live. Complete the sentences.

My city/state is _____.

Its geographic size is _____ square miles.

The number of people who live here is _____.

Here are some interesting facts about my city/state:

1. _____

2. _____

3. _____

4. _____

5. _____

Complete the luggage tag with **information** about you.

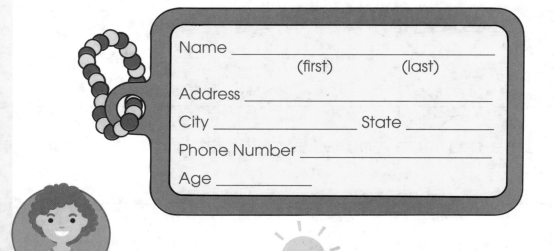

Name _____
            (first)   (last)

Address _____

City _____ State _____

Phone Number _____

Age _____

All About Me

Write to Inform

Choose a topic from the list. With an adult, research to learn facts about the topic. Complete the graphic organizer to plan an informative article. Write it on a separate sheet of paper.

| hurricanes | baking | reptiles |
| rain forests | Mt. Everest | U.S. presidents |

My topic is _____.

Introduction:

This topic is interesting or important because

_____.

Body:

Fact #1:_____

_____

Fact #2:_____

_____

Fact #3:_____

_____

Fact #4:_____

_____

Conclusion:

The most important thing for readers to remember about my topic is _____

_____.

Write an Opinion

Circle the statements that give opinions about each topic. Do not circle facts about the topics. To find the opinions, look for judgment words such as **good**, **better**, **worst**, **like**, and so on.

Watching TV is more fun than reading a book.

You can check out books from the library.

Reading a book is better than watching TV.

Beaches can be sandy or rocky.

A beach is the best place to go for vacation.

Sunburns, insects, and sand make trips to the beach annoying.

There is no tastier dessert than pie.

Cake is better than pie.

Some kinds of pies are fruit pies, cream pies, and meat pies.

Write an Opinion

What do you think is the best sport to play? Complete the sentence to state your opinion. Then, circle three good reasons for your opinion or write your own reasons.

The best sport to play is _____.

The reasons I think this are:

It is a team sport.

It is an individual sport.

It is good exercise.

It teaches you important lessons.

You do not need much equipment.

It is played outdoors.

It is played indoors.

It is easy to play.

It is challenging to play.

_____

_____

Write an Opinion

What makes a good friend? Complete the first sentence to state your opinion. Then, write three good reasons to support your opinion. Complete the last sentence as a conclusion to your opinion.

The most important way to be a good friend is to

_____

_____

_____.

Reason #1: _____

_____

Reason #2: _____

_____

Reason #3: _____

_____

Good friends are _____

_____.

Write an Opinion

Choose a topic from the list. Then, complete the graphic organizer to plan your writing. Write your complete opinion essay on a separate sheet of paper.

> the best way to exercise
> the best school subject
> the best dinner
>
> the best teacher you've ever had
> the best gift you've ever given
> the best game to play outside

Introduction:

The best _____ is

_____.

Body:

Reason #1: _____

_____

Reason #2: _____

_____

Reason #3: _____

_____

Conclusion:

Based on the evidence, people should agree with me that _____

_____.

Add to 20

Add. Do you see a pattern in the sums?

1 + 1 = ( )

6 + 6 = ( )

3 + 1 = ( )

8 + 6 = ( )

2 + 4 = ( )

9 + 7 = ( )

4 + 4 = ( )

10 + 8 = ( )

8 + 2 = ( )

10 + 10 = ( )

Subtract Within 20

Subtract. Do you see a pattern in the differences?

20 − 2 = ◯

16 − 8 = ◯

17 − 1 = ◯

18 − 12 = ◯

19 − 5 = ◯

19 − 15 = ◯

18 − 6 = ◯

10 − 8 = ◯

15 − 5 = ◯

10 − 10 = ◯

Addition Word Problems

Write an addition equation to solve each problem. Draw pictures to help you.

Rowan went to a pet shop with her dad. They bought 3 goldfish, 5 angelfish, and 5 guppies. How many fish did they buy in all?

_____ = _____ fish

Lucy went to the grocery store. She bought 4 jars of sauce, 8 boxes of pasta, and 3 rolls of paper towels. How many items did she buy in all?

_____ = _____ items

Choose a goal you want to achieve. It could be hitting a baseball, writing a story, doing a cartwheel, or something else. Write the number of times you practice each day for five days. **Add** to find the sum. Did you get closer to reaching your goal?

Day 1	Day 2	Day 3	Day 4	Day 5	Sum

Growth Mindset

Subtraction Word Problems

Write a subtraction equation to solve each problem. Draw pictures to help you.

Hayley baked 18 cupcakes. 2 cupcakes fell on the floor. Hayley's sister Kirsten took some cupcakes to her friends outside. Hayley has 11 cupcakes left. How many cupcakes did Kirsten take?

_____ = _____ cupcakes

Patrick earned 17 stickers on the reward chart this week. Richard earned 15 stickers. How many more stickers did Patrick earn?

_____ = _____ stickers

Cady and Coen collect marbles. In their collection of 20 marbles, 7 are striped and 4 are swirled. How many marbles are not striped or swirled?

_____ = _____ marbles

139

Add to 20

Add from memory.

$$\begin{array}{r} 10 \\ + \ 2 \\ \hline \end{array}$$
$$\begin{array}{r} 6 \\ + \ 7 \\ \hline \end{array}$$
$$\begin{array}{r} 11 \\ + \ 2 \\ \hline \end{array}$$
$$\begin{array}{r} 13 \\ + \ 1 \\ \hline \end{array}$$

$$\begin{array}{r} 16 \\ + \ 4 \\ \hline \end{array}$$
$$\begin{array}{r} 17 \\ + \ 1 \\ \hline \end{array}$$
$$\begin{array}{r} 12 \\ + \ 3 \\ \hline \end{array}$$
$$\begin{array}{r} 1 \\ + \ 1 \\ \hline \end{array}$$

$$\begin{array}{r} 15 \\ + \ 5 \\ \hline \end{array}$$
$$\begin{array}{r} 11 \\ + \ 8 \\ \hline \end{array}$$
$$\begin{array}{r} 5 \\ + \ 5 \\ \hline \end{array}$$
$$\begin{array}{r} 18 \\ + \ 2 \\ \hline \end{array}$$

Being a leader means using your skills to help others. With an adult, lead a collection of gently used clothes to donate to a charity in your community. **Add** the items you collected. Finish the sentence.

I helped collect _____ items for people in need.

Subtract Within 20

Subtract from memory.

$$\begin{array}{r} 13 \\ -\ 3 \\ \hline \end{array} \qquad \begin{array}{r} 4 \\ -\ 1 \\ \hline \end{array} \qquad \begin{array}{r} 5 \\ -\ 2 \\ \hline \end{array} \qquad \begin{array}{r} 15 \\ -\ 6 \\ \hline \end{array}$$

$$\begin{array}{r} 11 \\ -\ 7 \\ \hline \end{array} \qquad \begin{array}{r} 19 \\ -12 \\ \hline \end{array} \qquad \begin{array}{r} 14 \\ -\ 7 \\ \hline \end{array} \qquad \begin{array}{r} 16 \\ -15 \\ \hline \end{array}$$

$$\begin{array}{r} 15 \\ -\ 4 \\ \hline \end{array} \qquad \begin{array}{r} 19 \\ -\ 8 \\ \hline \end{array} \qquad \begin{array}{r} 3 \\ -\ 2 \\ \hline \end{array} \qquad \begin{array}{r} 14 \\ -10 \\ \hline \end{array}$$

$$\begin{array}{r} 17 \\ -11 \\ \hline \end{array} \qquad \begin{array}{r} 18 \\ -\ 4 \\ \hline \end{array} \qquad \begin{array}{r} 16 \\ -\ 4 \\ \hline \end{array} \qquad \begin{array}{r} 12 \\ -\ 9 \\ \hline \end{array}$$

141

Add & Subtract Within 20

Add or subtract from memory.

<table>
<tr><td>13
− 7</td><td>6
+ 1</td><td>8
− 3</td><td>14
+ 6</td></tr>
<tr><td>19
−15</td><td>15
+ 2</td><td>14
+ 2</td><td>11
− 7</td></tr>
<tr><td>8
+ 8</td><td>15
− 8</td><td>13
− 5</td><td>18
+ 2</td></tr>
<tr><td>17
−15</td><td>8
+ 9</td><td>14
− 9</td><td>3
+ 6</td></tr>
</table>

Addition & Subtraction Word Problems

Read each problem. Write whether you should add or subtract. Then, solve.

7 fans were cheering for the Bears. 11 fans were cheering for the Comets. How many fans were cheering in all?

Add or subtract? _____   _____ fans

Isabella's hair was 18 inches long. After a haircut, her hair was 9 inches long. How much of Isabella's hair got cut off?

Add or subtract? _____   _____ inches

9 children were on the bus. At the bus stop, 7 more children got on. How many children were riding the bus in all?

Add or subtract? _____   _____ children

14 birds were perched in a tree. A dog barked, and 4 birds flew away. How many birds were left in the tree?

Add or subtract? _____   _____ birds

Count by Twos

Count each group of objects by twos. Circle an answer to the question for each group. The first one is done for you.

$$\underline{2} \quad \underline{4} \quad \underline{6} \quad \underline{8} \quad \underline{10} \quad \underline{12} \quad \underline{14} \quad \underline{15}$$

Can the group be counted evenly by twos?   Yes   (No)

____ ____ ____ ____ ____

Can the group be counted evenly by twos?   Yes   No

____ ____ ____ ____ ____

Can the group be counted evenly by twos?   Yes   No

144

Count by Twos

Circle pairs in each group of objects. Then, count the objects by twos and answer the questions.

How many pairs did you circle? _____

Can the group be counted evenly by twos?   **Yes**   **No**

How many pairs did you circle? _____

Can the group be counted evenly by twos?   **Yes**   **No**

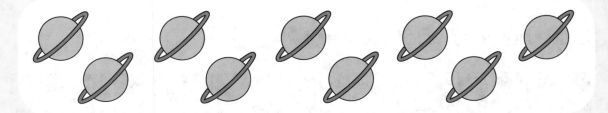

How many pairs did you circle? _____

Can the group be counted evenly by twos?   **Yes**   **No**

Odd & Even Numbers

You can count to an even number evenly by twos. When you count odd numbers by twos, there is 1 left over. Count the objects in each group by twos. Write the total number of objects in the group. Then, tell whether the number is odd or even.

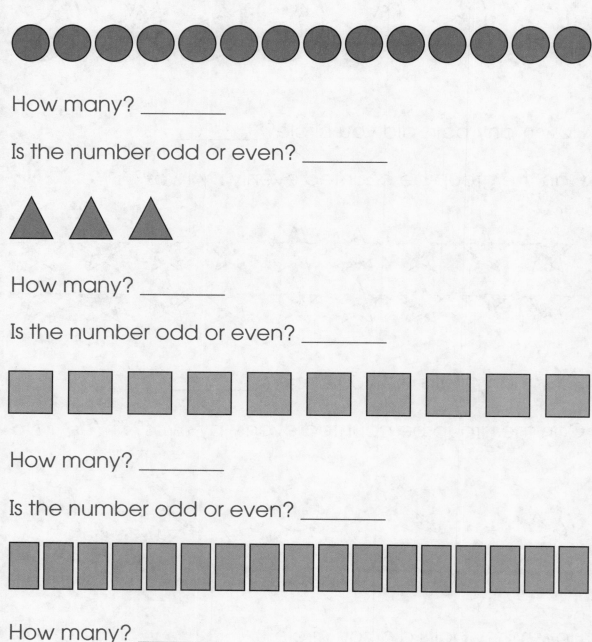

How many? _____

Is the number odd or even? _____

How many? _____

Is the number odd or even? _____

How many? _____

Is the number odd or even? _____

How many? _____

Is the number odd or even? _____

Odd & Even Numbers

Color an even number of shapes in each group.

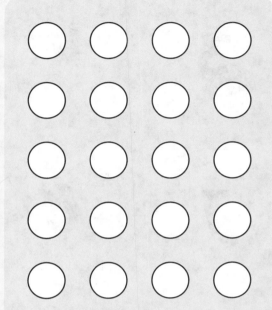
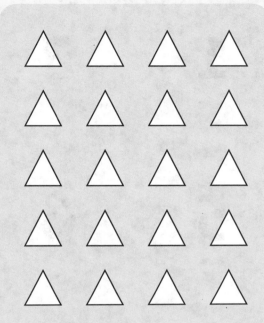

Color an odd number of shapes in each group.

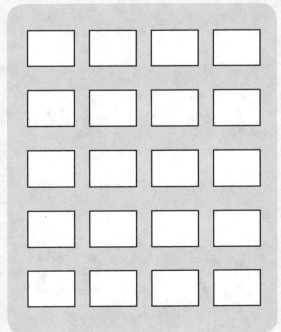

Odd & Even Numbers

Color the even numbers orange. Color the odd numbers blue.

1	2	3	4
5	6	7	8
9	10	11	12
13	14	15	16
17	18	19	20

Odd & Even Numbers

Even numbers end with **0**, **2**, **4**, **6**, or **8**. Odd numbers end with **1**, **3**, **5**, **7**, or **9**. Circle the even numbers.

Circle the odd numbers.

Write your age. Then, write what your age will be in future years. Circle the ages that are **even** numbers. Draw a box around the ages that are **odd** numbers.

This year, I am _____ years old.

In 2025, I will be _____ years old.

In 2026, I will be _____ years old.

In 2030, I will be _____ years old.

Arrays

Look at each group of insects. Write an equation to find the sum of the insects in rows. Then, write an equation to find the sum of the insects in columns. The first one is done for you.

Column ↓
Row →

$$\underline{4} + \underline{4} = \underline{8}$$

$$\underline{2} + \underline{2} + \underline{2} + \underline{2} = \underline{8}$$

$$\underline{} + \underline{} + \underline{} = \underline{}$$

$$\underline{} + \underline{} + \underline{} + \underline{} = \underline{}$$

$$\underline{} + \underline{} + \underline{} + \underline{} + \underline{} = \underline{}$$

$$\underline{} + \underline{} + \underline{} = \underline{}$$

$$\underline{} + \underline{} + \underline{} = \underline{}$$

$$\underline{} + \underline{} + \underline{} = \underline{}$$

150

Arrays

Draw a group of dots to illustrate each pair of addition problems. The first one is done for you.

Rows: 4 + 4 + 4 + 4 + 4 = 20
Columns: 5 + 5 + 5 + 5 = 20

Rows: 5 + 5 + 5 + 5 = 20
Columns: 4 + 4 + 4 + 4 + 4 = 20

Rows: 3 + 3 = 6
Columns: 2 + 2 + 2 = 6

Rows: 5 + 5 + 5 + 5 + 5 = 25
Columns: 5 + 5 + 5 + 5 + 5 = 25

Regroup

When the sum of the digits in the ones column is more than 10, regroup 10 ones as 1 ten. Solve each problem. Draw the regrouped tens blocks and ones blocks. The first one is done for you.

17
+14
31

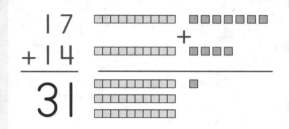

38
+26

45
+45

64
+18

Regroup

When there are not enough ones to subtract from, regroup 1 ten as 10 ones. Solve each problem. Draw the regrouped tens blocks and ones blocks for the minuend, or number being subtracted from. Then, cross out the subtrahend, or number being subtracted. The first one is done for you.

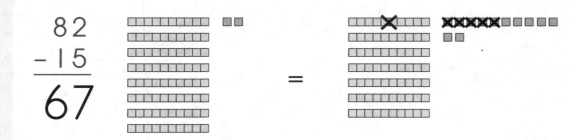

$$\begin{array}{r} 82 \\ -15 \\ \hline 67 \end{array}$$

$$\begin{array}{r} 35 \\ -29 \\ \hline \end{array}$$

$$\begin{array}{r} 71 \\ -56 \\ \hline \end{array}$$

$$\begin{array}{r} 43 \\ -9 \\ \hline \end{array}$$

Add Two-Digit Numbers

Add. Regroup 10 ones as 1 ten.

23 +18	34 +39	56 +24	67 +24
53 +28	15 +25	36 +45	76 +15
47 +27	45 +55	62 +19	48 +13
33 +27	56 +25	34 +27	17 +26

Addition Word Problems

Read and solve.

Bobby's Bake Shop sold 57 cakes last week. This week, the shop sold 39 cakes. How many cakes did the shop sell during the two weeks?

_____ cakes

A farmer has 68 chicken eggs and 24 duck eggs. How many eggs does the farmer have in all?

_____ eggs

Finley has two apple trees in her backyard. One tree has 42 apples. The other tree has 38 apples. How many apples are on the trees in Finley's backyard?

_____ apples

Work with a partner. Think about what the two of you have in common. The ideas below will get you started. **Add** all the things you have in common and write the sum.

pets	friends	favorite sports
families	toys	favorite foods
hobbies	interests	favorite movies

We have _____ things in common!

Social Skills

Subtract Two-Digit Numbers

Subtract. Regroup 1 ten as 10 ones.

$$\begin{array}{r} 82 \\ -69 \\ \hline \end{array} \qquad \begin{array}{r} 73 \\ -36 \\ \hline \end{array} \qquad \begin{array}{r} 25 \\ -17 \\ \hline \end{array} \qquad \begin{array}{r} 76 \\ -37 \\ \hline \end{array}$$

$$\begin{array}{r} 88 \\ -19 \\ \hline \end{array} \qquad \begin{array}{r} 58 \\ -39 \\ \hline \end{array} \qquad \begin{array}{r} 27 \\ -18 \\ \hline \end{array} \qquad \begin{array}{r} 57 \\ -18 \\ \hline \end{array}$$

$$\begin{array}{r} 37 \\ -27 \\ \hline \end{array} \qquad \begin{array}{r} 71 \\ -56 \\ \hline \end{array} \qquad \begin{array}{r} 36 \\ -18 \\ \hline \end{array} \qquad \begin{array}{r} 40 \\ -21 \\ \hline \end{array}$$

$$\begin{array}{r} 51 \\ -24 \\ \hline \end{array} \qquad \begin{array}{r} 36 \\ -27 \\ \hline \end{array} \qquad \begin{array}{r} 82 \\ -44 \\ \hline \end{array} \qquad \begin{array}{r} 62 \\ -15 \\ \hline \end{array}$$

Subtraction Word Problems

Read and solve.

28 students in Sam's class played Bingo on a rainy day. 19 of those students won a prize. How many students did not win a prize?

_____ students

Ms. Taylor scooped 45 scoops of ice cream for the children at her son's birthday party. At the end of the party, 16 scoops had not been eaten. How many scoops of ice cream were eaten?

_____ scoops

Bryn took a walk around the pond. She saw 14 frogs and 34 birds. On her second loop around the pond, she counted 19 birds. How many birds had flown away?

_____ birds

To be a good listener, do four things: look into the person's eyes, lean slightly forward, nod and say things like "uh-huh," and ask questions. Ask a friend to talk while you do all these things. Then, one by one, **subtract** each behavior. How does your friend feel each time? Take turns to see how you feel when someone is and is not a good listener.

Add & Subtract Two-Digit Numbers

Add or subtract. Regroup as needed.

$$
\begin{array}{r} 41 \\ +56 \\ \hline \end{array}
\qquad
\begin{array}{r} 90 \\ -45 \\ \hline \end{array}
\qquad
\begin{array}{r} 76 \\ +12 \\ \hline \end{array}
\qquad
\begin{array}{r} 59 \\ -34 \\ \hline \end{array}
$$

$$
\begin{array}{r} 95 \\ -63 \\ \hline \end{array}
\qquad
\begin{array}{r} 43 \\ +17 \\ \hline \end{array}
\qquad
\begin{array}{r} 82 \\ -56 \\ \hline \end{array}
\qquad
\begin{array}{r} 63 \\ -40 \\ \hline \end{array}
$$

$$
\begin{array}{r} 68 \\ -29 \\ \hline \end{array}
\qquad
\begin{array}{r} 32 \\ +33 \\ \hline \end{array}
\qquad
\begin{array}{r} 51 \\ +19 \\ \hline \end{array}
\qquad
\begin{array}{r} 69 \\ -47 \\ \hline \end{array}
$$

$$
\begin{array}{r} 76 \\ -30 \\ \hline \end{array}
\qquad
\begin{array}{r} 57 \\ -19 \\ \hline \end{array}
\qquad
\begin{array}{r} 67 \\ +20 \\ \hline \end{array}
\qquad
\begin{array}{r} 86 \\ +11 \\ \hline \end{array}
$$

Addition & Subtraction Word Problems

Read each problem. Write whether you should add or subtract. Then, solve.

One fawn weighs 54 pounds. Her brother weighs 43 pounds. How much do they weigh in all?

Add or subtract? _____ _____ pounds

Mr. McDaniel had a box of 60 crayons. Zac took 12 crayons. How many crayons were left in the box?

Add or subtract? _____ _____ crayons

Eliza started with 52 cards. Willie took 13 cards. Adam took 11 cards. How many cards did Eliza have left?

Add or subtract? _____ _____ cards

Place Value

A number with three digits is made up of ones, tens, and hundreds. In the number **234**, **4** is in the ones place. Its value is 4 ones, or 4. The digit **3** is in the tens place. Its value is 3 tens, or 30. The digit **2** is in the hundreds place. Its value is 2 hundreds, or 200. Write the number shown by each group of hundreds, tens, and ones blocks. The first one is done for you.

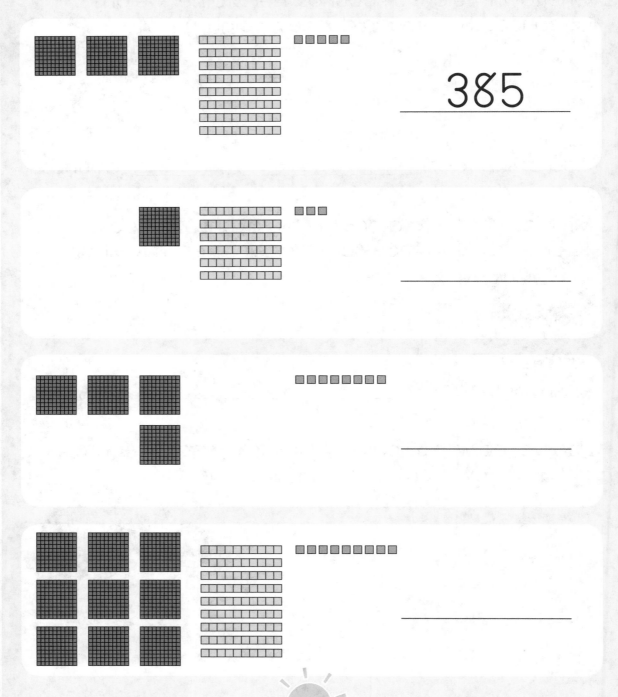

385

Place Value

Write the number shown by each group of hundreds, tens, and ones blocks.

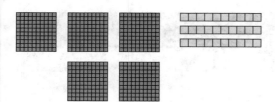

_____

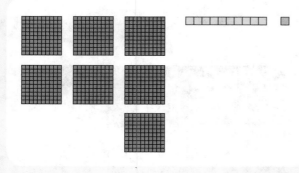

_____

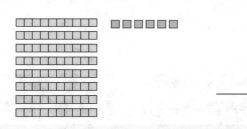

_____

_____

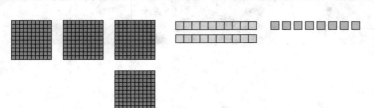

_____

Place Value

Write the number of hundreds, tens, and ones for each number.

250

Hundreds	Tens	Ones

342

Hundreds	Tens	Ones

876

Hundreds	Tens	Ones

945

Hundreds	Tens	Ones

515

Hundreds	Tens	Ones

174

Hundreds	Tens	Ones

801

Hundreds	Tens	Ones

679

Hundreds	Tens	Ones

Place Value

Write the value of the underlined digit. The first three are done for you.

6̲5 __**60**__   2̲35 __**200**__   831̲ __**1**__

479̲ _____   2̲3 _____   5̲80 _____

5̲12 _____   68̲4 _____   70̲3 _____

34̲7 _____   5̲83 _____   16̲9 _____

To **value** something means to believe that it has great worth or importance. What do you value most? It could be friends, family, pets, sports, music, or something else. Draw and write on the T-shirts to show what you value.

Character Development

Place Value

Use the code to color the numbers.

Color the number with 4 tens and 8 ones **red**.

Color the number with 3 hundreds and 7 tens blue.

Color the number with 9 hundreds and 6 ones **green**.

Color the number with 1 ten and 7 ones yellow.

Color the number with 8 hundreds and 3 tens orange.

Color the number with 7 hundreds **purple**.

Color the number with 5 tens pink.

Color the number with 3 ones **brown**.

648   780

371

51   986

117

463   836

Place Value

Look at each group of hundreds, tens, and ones blocks. Complete the sentences.

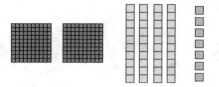

The number shown is _____.

It has _____ hundreds, _____ tens, and _____ ones.

The value of the digit in the hundreds place is _____.

The value of the digit in the tens place is _____.

The value of the digit in the ones place is _____.

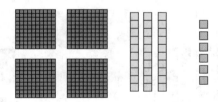

The number shown is _____.

It has _____ hundreds, _____ tens, and _____ ones.

The value of the digit in the hundreds place is _____.

The value of the digit in the tens place is _____.

The value of the digit in the ones place is _____.

Expanded Form

Expanded form is a way to write a number by adding the values of its digits. Look at each number. Complete its expanded form. The first one is done for you.

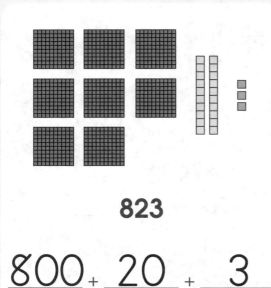

823

$\underline{800} + \underline{20} + \underline{3}$

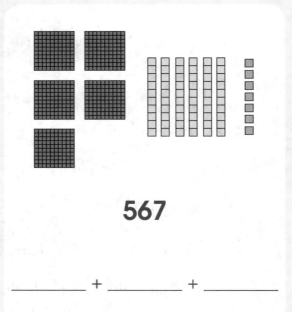

567

_____ + _____ + _____

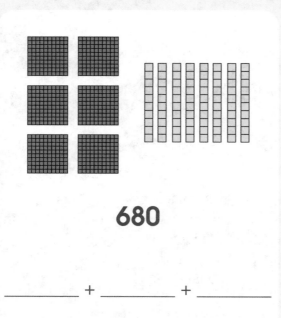

680

_____ + _____ + _____

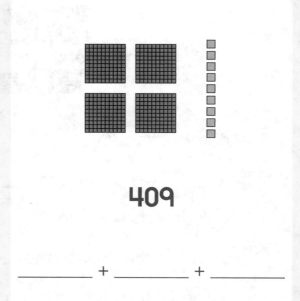

409

_____ + _____ + _____

Expanded Form

Look at each expanded form. Circle the matching number.

500 + 80 + 6

586

568

580

200 + 30

203

233

230

400 + 10 + 2

410

412

421

900 + 50 + 7

907

957

975

800 + 4

840

804

844

70 + 5

705

750

75

Look at each number. Circle its expanded form.

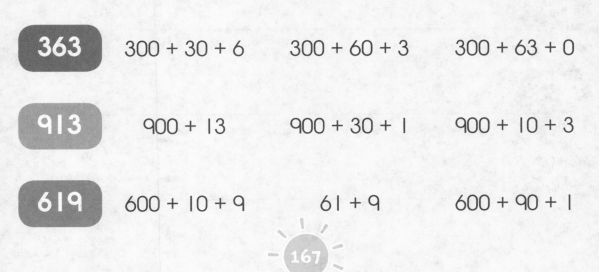

363   300 + 30 + 6   300 + 60 + 3   300 + 63 + 0

913   900 + 13   900 + 30 + 1   900 + 10 + 3

619   600 + 10 + 9   61 + 9   600 + 90 + 1

Expanded Form

Write each number in expanded form.

144 _____

460 _____

73 _____

347 _____

675 _____

68 _____

942 _____

473 _____

999 _____

Expanded Form

Complete the chart.

Standard Form	Expanded Form
84	
	900 + 20 + 1
635	
	800 + 60 + 6
99	
612	
	700 + 9
	200 + 20 + 8

Number Names

Match the numbers and words.

two hundred fifty-four

six

seven hundred
twenty-seven

five hundred ninety-eight

sixty-seven

Number Names

Cut out the numbers. Tape or glue them in the boxes to complete the chart.

Hundreds	Tens	Ones

two hundred seventy-eight

four hundred twenty-three

five hundred seventeen

six hundred fifty-eight

one hundred thirty-six

nine hundred forty-nine

1	2	3	4	5	6	7	8	9
1	2	3	4	5	6	7	8	9

BLANK PAGE FOR CUTTING ACTIVITY

Number Names

Write the name of each number. Do not use the word **and**. If the number has 2 or more tens and more than 0 ones, use a hyphen (-) between the words that name them. The first two are done for you.

563 five hundred sixty-three

419 four hundred nineteen

83 _____

751 _____

806 _____

920 _____

Write Numbers Three Ways

Complete the number pyramids. The first one is done for you.

562

500 + 60 + 2

five hundred sixty-two

484

_____

four hundred eighty-four

_____

900 + 10 + 1

nine hundred eleven

Write Numbers Three Ways

Complete the number pyramids.

_____

_____

eight hundred four

668

600 + 60 + 8

_____

779

700 + 70 + 9

_____

Compare Numbers

In each row, circle the number that is the greatest. Draw a box around the number that is the least.

699	609	96	669	69

290	219	291	209	289

348	83	388	384	303

129	212	199	292	229

503	53	500	305	553

Compare Numbers

The symbol > means "greater than."
The symbol < means "less than."
The symbol = means "equal to."
Cut out the numbers. Tape or glue
them in the boxes to make true
comparisons.

☐	< 567	☐	> 809
☐	> 450	☐	= 541
☐	< 499	☐	< 203
☐	= 321	☐	> 652
☐	= 128	☐	> 745

321	541	128	821	789
675	526	497	200	465

BLANK PAGE FOR CUTTING ACTIVITY

Compare Numbers

Write <, >, or = in each circle.

366 ◯ 929   581 ◯ 259   928 ◯ 172

163 ◯ 642   545 ◯ 501   445 ◯ 466

600 + 40 + 8 ◯ six hundred fifty-eight

800 + 70 + 7 ◯ 800 + 7

900 + 20 + 7 ◯ 900 + 20 + 7

one hundred fifty-five ◯ 100 + 50 + 1

six hundred eighty-seven ◯ 600 + 70 + 8

Count by Ones

Count forward and backward by ones from the numbers shown. Write the missing numbers.

699 ___ 701 ___ ___

___ 316 ___ ___ 319

569 ___ ___ ___ 573

___ ___ ___ 999 1,000

Count by Fives

Count forward and backward by fives from the numbers shown.
Write the missing numbers.

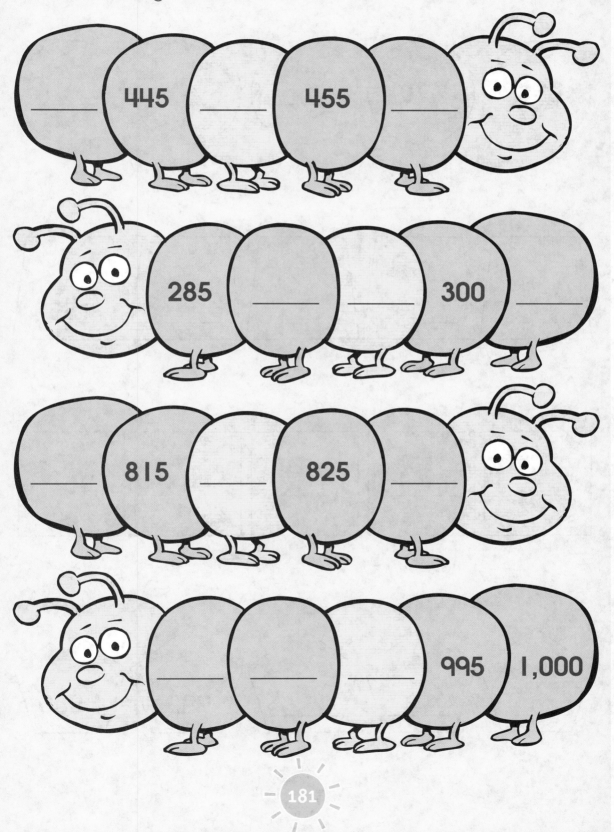

Count by Tens

Count forward and backward by tens from the numbers shown.
Write the missing numbers.

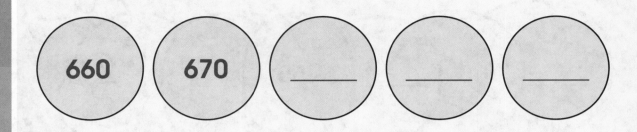

660   670   _____   _____   _____

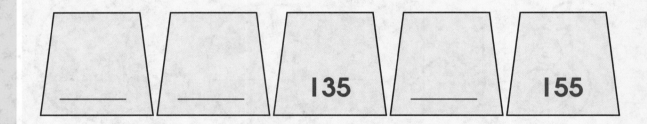

_____   _____   135   _____   155

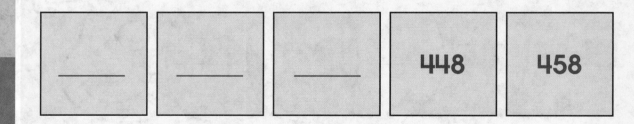

_____   _____   _____   448   458

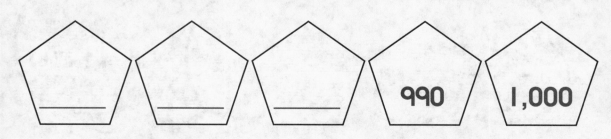

_____   _____   _____   990   1,000

Count by Hundreds

Count forward and backward by hundreds from the numbers shown. Write the missing numbers.

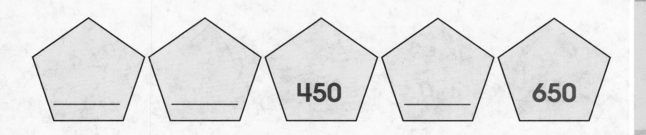

| 300 | 400 | _____ | _____ | _____ |

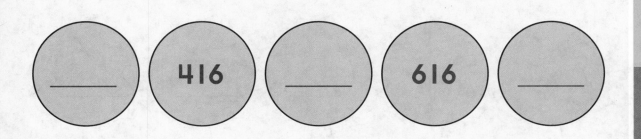

_____   _____   450   _____   650

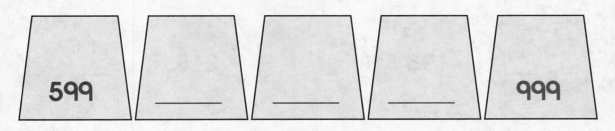

_____   416   _____   616   _____

599   _____   _____   _____   999

Number Patterns

Decide if each pattern shows counting by ones, fives, tens, or hundreds. Write the missing numbers.

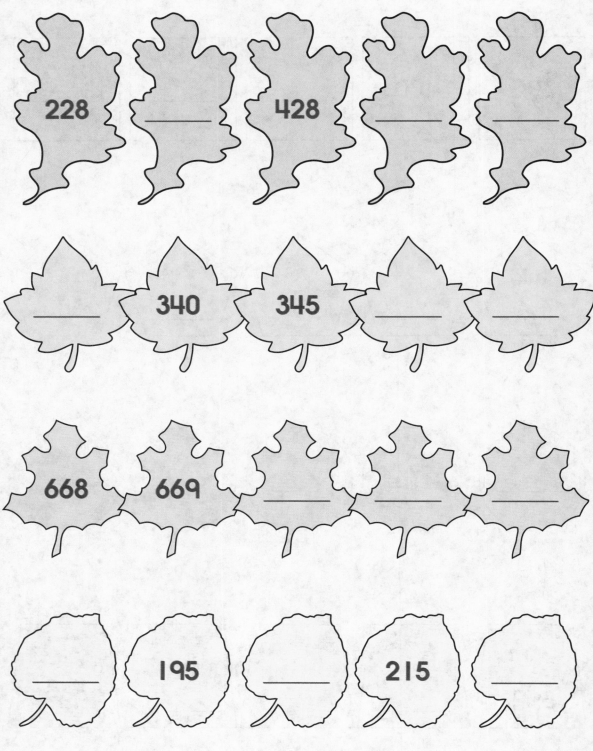

228 ____ 428 ____ ____

____ 340 345 ____ ____

668 669 ____ ____ ____

____ 195 ____ 215 ____

184

Number Patterns

Decide if each pattern shows counting by ones, fives, tens, or hundreds. Write the missing numbers.

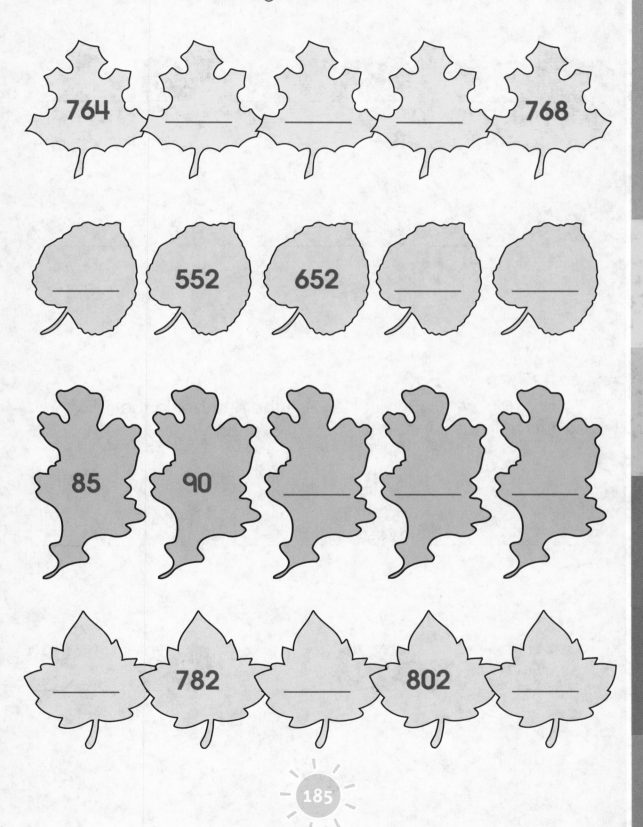

764 _____ _____ _____ 768

_____ 552 652 _____ _____

85 90 _____ _____ _____

_____ 782 _____ 802 _____

Add & Subtract 10

Add 10 to each number. Use the number in the tens place to help you. It is **red**.

24 _____   245 _____   675 _____

18 _____   58 _____   367 _____

Subtract 10 from each number. Use the number in the tens place to help you. It is **red**.

132 _____   456 _____   670 _____

350 _____   610 _____   775 _____

Add & Subtract 10

Look at each number. Write the numbers that are 10 more and 10 less.

−10 **+10**

334

−10 **+10**
78

−10 **+10**

526

−10 **+10**
851

−10 **+10**

645

−10 **+10**
269

Add & Subtract 100

Add 100 to each number. Use the number in the hundreds place to help you. It is **green**. One number does not have a **green** digit. Why not?

579 _____   324 _____   104 _____

341 _____   46 _____   325 _____

Subtract 100 from each number. Use the number in the hundreds place to help you. It is **green**.

146 _____   345 _____   214 _____

769 _____   645 _____   462 _____

Add & Subtract 100

Look at each number. Write the numbers that are 100 more and 100 less.

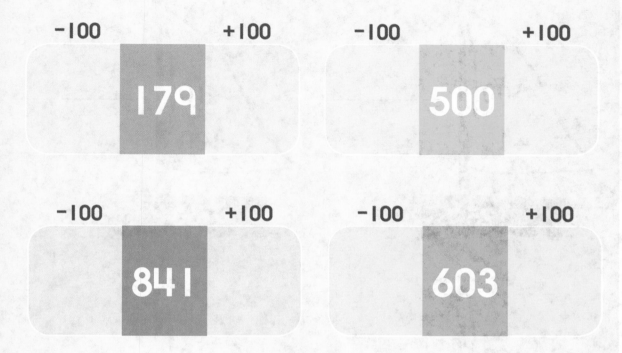

−100		+100		−100		+100
	179				500	

−100		+100		−100		+100
	841				603	

Some people collect rocks, stickers, action figures, or postcards. What collection of **100** things would you like to have? Write about it. Then, draw three things that might be in your collection.

My collection of 100 things would be _____

_____.

All About Me

Add & Subtract 10 or 100

Start with the number on each boat. Follow the directions on the sails to add and subtract.

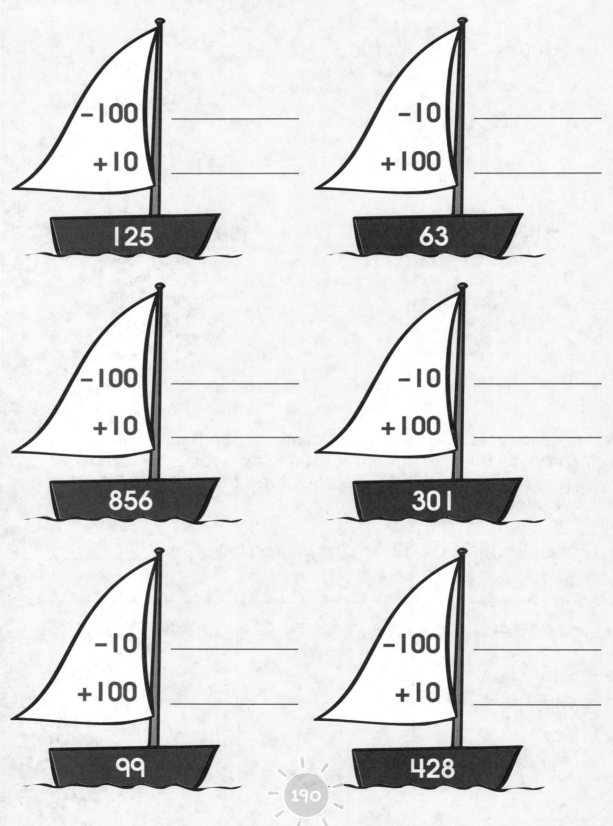

−100
+10
_____
_____
125

−10
+100
_____
_____
63

−100
+10
_____
_____
856

−10
+100
_____
_____
301

−10
+100
_____
_____
99

−100
+10
_____
_____
428

Add & Subtract 10 or 100

Follow the directions in each box.

850	
Add 10.	Subtract 10.
Add 100.	Subtract 100.

625	
Add 10.	Subtract 10.
Add 100.	Subtract 100.

231	
Add 10.	Subtract 10.
Add 100.	Subtract 100.

206	
Add 10.	Subtract 10.
Add 100.	Subtract 100.

790	
Add 10.	Subtract 10.
Add 100.	Subtract 100.

531	
Add 10.	Subtract 10.
Add 100.	Subtract 100.

Add Two-Digit Numbers

Add. In each problem, regroup 10 ones as 1 ten or 20 ones as 2 tens. Two are done for you.

```
            1
  85       24       63       78
  54       56       25       45
 +25      +78      +35      +68
          158
```

```
                              2
  53       35       25       35
  35       23       85       76
  46       56       55       86
 +38      +35      +24      +58
                            255
```

```
  77       54       21       76
  75       89       56       35
  65       87       11       95
 +13      +26      +89      +25
```

Add Two-Digit Numbers

Add. Color the matching sums on the flag.

55	56	68	32	79
30	41	90	35	97
+78	+36	+10	24	51
			+89	+79

12	71	87	96	56
45	53	54	35	41
78	84	42	25	38
+69	+62	+78	+70	+72

168	514	133	328
840	306	609	226
163	206	180	145
302	204	840	207
270	708	261	908

Add Three-Digit Numbers

First, add the ones. Next, add the tens. Last, add the hundreds.

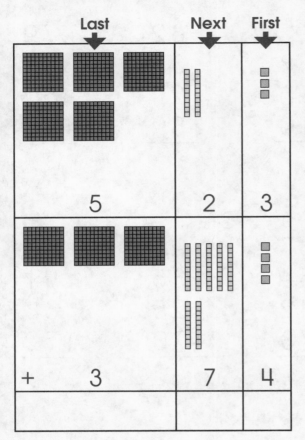

Last	Next	First		Last	Next	First
5	2	3		4	5	6
+ 3	7	4		+ 2	4	3

$$\begin{array}{r} 291 \\ +707 \\ \hline \end{array}$$ $$\begin{array}{r} 170 \\ +829 \\ \hline \end{array}$$ $$\begin{array}{r} 632 \\ +335 \\ \hline \end{array}$$

$$\begin{array}{r} 733 \\ +266 \\ \hline \end{array}$$ $$\begin{array}{r} 208 \\ +591 \\ \hline \end{array}$$ $$\begin{array}{r} 282 \\ +617 \\ \hline \end{array}$$

Add Three-Digit Numbers

Add. Draw a line to complete each equation.

166 + 210 =

770

825 + 164 =

376

407 + 191 =

989

550 + 220 =

598

732 + 145 =

877

Subtract Three-Digit Numbers

First, subtract the ones. Next, subtract the tens. Last, subtract the hundreds.

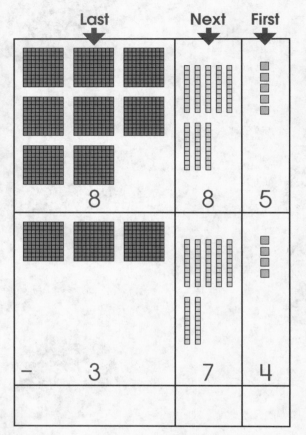

```
  357        437        568
 -142       -416       -235
 _____      _____      _____


  389        869        758
 -341       -542       -214
 _____      _____      _____
```

Subtract Three-Digit Numbers

Subtract. Draw a line to complete each equation.

748 – 326 =

984 – 651 =

635 – 521 =

269 – 130 =

879 – 452 =

333

427

139

422

114

Subtract the word **not** from each sentence. Then, read the statements about learning and trying hard. Which one can you tell yourself today?

It is not OK to make mistakes.

This is not getting easier every day.

I will not keep trying to reach my goals.

Learning this is not possible.

Growth Mindset

Regroup

When the sum of the ones is more than 10, regroup 10 ones as 1 ten. When the sum of the tens is more than 10, regroup 10 tens as 1 hundred. Solve each problem. Draw the regrouped hundreds, tens, and ones blocks. The first one is done for you.

$$\begin{array}{r} 259 \\ +469 \\ \hline 728 \end{array}$$

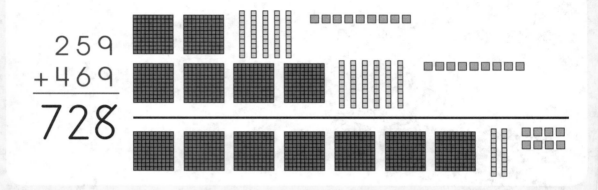

$$\begin{array}{r} 427 \\ +181 \\ \hline \end{array}$$

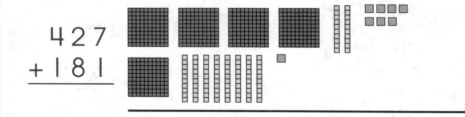

$$\begin{array}{r} 863 \\ +56 \\ \hline \end{array}$$

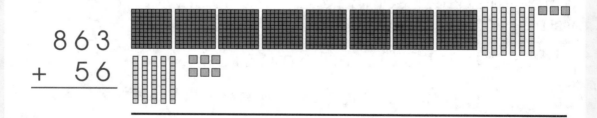

Add Three-Digit Numbers

Add. Regroup 10 ones as 1 ten. Regroup 10 tens as 1 hundred. Two are done for you.

```
  258        425        744
+ 467      + 489      + 207
```

```
  423         1          642
+ 257        734       + 319
            + 149
            ────
             883
```

```
  1 1
  152        536        437
+ 348      + 128      + 268
────
 500
```

```
  523        366        618
+ 427      + 235      + 349
```

199

Add Three-Digit Numbers

Add. Write the missing numbers.

```
   ◯ 1 3          2 1 5          1 2 4
 + 2 ◯ 9        + 5 ◯ 7        + 5 3 ◯
 ─────────      ─────────      ─────────
   3 7 2          7 4 ◯          ◯ 6 2


   1 9 4          ◯ 5 4          3 ◯ 3
 + 6 ◯ 8        + 3 4 9        + 3 4 7
 ─────────      ─────────      ─────────
   ◯ 5 2          7 0 ◯          ◯ 7 0


   2 1 4          6 7 ◯          ◯ 2 3
 + ◯ 5 8        + 1 3 8        + 7 6 5
 ─────────      ─────────      ─────────
   8 7 ◯          8 ◯ 2          9 8 ◯
```

Regroup

When there are not enough ones to subtract from, regroup 1 ten as 10 ones. When there are not enough tens to subtract from, regroup 1 hundred as 10 tens. Solve each problem. Draw the regrouped hundreds blocks, tens blocks, and ones blocks for the minuend, or number being subtracted from. Then, cross out the subtrahend, or number being subtracted. The first one is done for you.

$$\begin{array}{r} 7\ 3\ 2 \\ -\ 1\ 5\ 9 \\ \hline 5\ 7\ 3 \end{array}$$

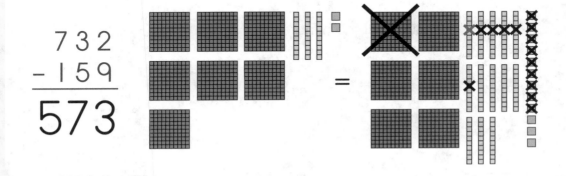

$$\begin{array}{r} 8\ 2\ 6 \\ -\ 4\ 6\ 3 \end{array}$$

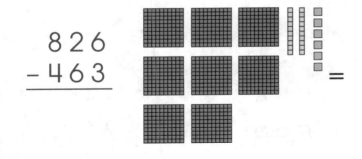

$$\begin{array}{r} 7\ 1\ 1 \\ -\ 6\ 5\ 3 \end{array}$$

Subtract Three-Digit Numbers

Subtract. If needed, regroup 1 ten as 10 ones. Regroup 1 hundred as 10 tens. Follow the example.

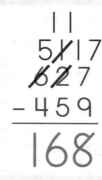

1. Subtract the ones. 9 ones cannot be subtracted from 7 ones. Regroup 1 ten as 10 ones: 17 − 9 = **8**. Only 1 ten is left.

2. Subtract the tens. 5 tens cannot be subtracted from 1 ten. Regroup 1 hundred as 10 tens: 11 − 5 = **6**. Only 5 hundreds are left.

3. Subtract the hundreds: 5 − 4 = **1**.

$$\begin{array}{r} 832 \\ -627 \\ \hline \end{array}$$

$$\begin{array}{r} 475 \\ -228 \\ \hline \end{array}$$

$$\begin{array}{r} 597 \\ -459 \\ \hline \end{array}$$

$$\begin{array}{r} 638 \\ -219 \\ \hline \end{array}$$

$$\begin{array}{r} 944 \\ -635 \\ \hline \end{array}$$

$$\begin{array}{r} 383 \\ -267 \\ \hline \end{array}$$

$$\begin{array}{r} 347 \\ -239 \\ \hline \end{array}$$

$$\begin{array}{r} 932 \\ -703 \\ \hline \end{array}$$

$$\begin{array}{r} 861 \\ -102 \\ \hline \end{array}$$

Subtract Three-Digit Numbers

Subtract. Regroup as needed. Use the code to color the flowers.

If the difference has 1 one, color it **red**.
If the difference has 5 ones, color it yellow.
If the difference has 7 ones, color it **purple**.
If the difference has 8 ones, color it pink.

Add & Subtract Three-Digit Numbers

Add or subtract. Regroup when needed.

I hundred = 10 tens   I ten = 10 ones

$$
\begin{array}{r} 762 \\ +234 \\ \hline \end{array}
\qquad
\begin{array}{r} 658 \\ -153 \\ \hline \end{array}
\qquad
\begin{array}{r} 658 \\ -423 \\ \hline \end{array}
\qquad
\begin{array}{r} 769 \\ -357 \\ \hline \end{array}
$$

$$
\begin{array}{r} 278 \\ -120 \\ \hline \end{array}
\qquad
\begin{array}{r} 254 \\ +556 \\ \hline \end{array}
\qquad
\begin{array}{r} 538 \\ +124 \\ \hline \end{array}
\qquad
\begin{array}{r} 781 \\ +201 \\ \hline \end{array}
$$

Addition & Subtraction Word Problems

Read and solve.

Eva goes to school 185 days each year. Yoko goes to school 313 days each year. How many more days of school does Yoko attend each year?

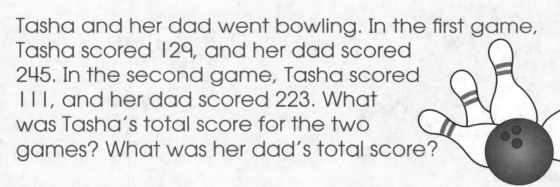

_____ days

Tasha and her dad went bowling. In the first game, Tasha scored 129, and her dad scored 245. In the second game, Tasha scored 111, and her dad scored 223. What was Tasha's total score for the two games? What was her dad's total score?

Tasha's total score: _____

Tasha's dad's total score: _____

What can you **subtract** from your day to make it better? It could be playing too many video games or fighting with your brother or sister. What can you **add** to your day to make it better? It could be playing outside or doing something nice for someone you know.

Measure in Inches

Look at the kangaroo's foot. It is three inches long. Use a ruler to measure the length of each animal's foot to the nearest inch.

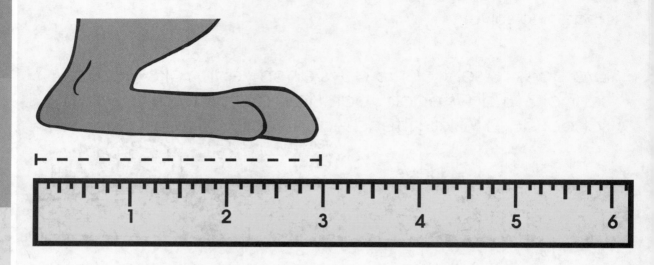

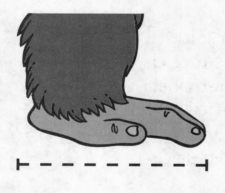

_____ inches

_____ inch

_____ inch

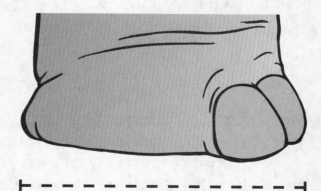

_____ inches

Measure in Inches

Estimate the length of each object in inches. Then, use a ruler to measure each object to the nearest inch.

	Estimated Length	Actual Length
your foot	_____	_____
your hand	_____	_____
toothbrush	_____	_____
fork	_____	_____
drinking glass	_____	_____
paper clip	_____	_____
your shoe	_____	_____

Try to touch your toes without bending your knees. If you cannot reach your toes, ask a friend to use a ruler to measure how many more **inches** you still need to stretch. Practice for five days. Then, measure again. Did you become more flexible and get closer to your goal?

Health & Fitness

Inches & Feet

Most rulers are one foot long. There are 12 inches in one foot. Write **inches** or **feet** below each object to tell whether you would measure its length in inches or in feet.

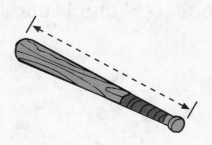

_____

_____

_____

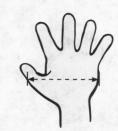

_____

_____

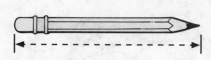

_____

_____

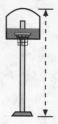

_____

Measure in Centimeters

A centimeter measures length in the metric system. There are about two and one-half centimeters in one inch. Look at the kangaroo's foot. It is eight centimeters long. Find a ruler that has centimeters. Use it to measure the length of each animal's foot to the nearest centimeter.

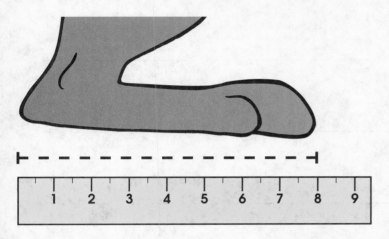

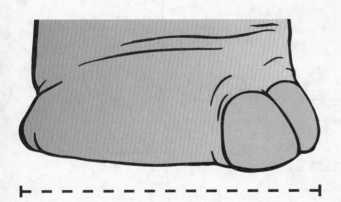

_____ centimeters

_____ centimeters

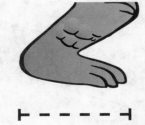

_____ centimeters

_____ centimeters

Measure in Centimeters

Estimate the length of each object in centimeters. Then, use a ruler to measure each object to the nearest centimeter.

	Estimated Length	Actual Length
your foot	_____	_____
your hand	_____	_____
toothbrush	_____	_____
fork	_____	_____
drinking glass	_____	_____
paper clip	_____	_____
your shoe	_____	_____

Centimeters & Meters

There are 100 centimeters in one meter. Write **centimeters** or **meters** beside each object to tell whether you would measure its length in centimeters or in meters.

_____

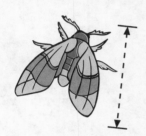

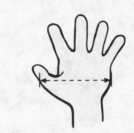

_____

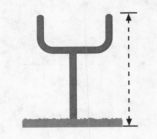

_____

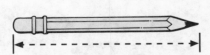

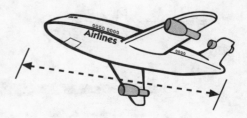

_____

Inches & Centimeters

Measure the length of each object to the nearest inch. Measure it again to the nearest centimeter.

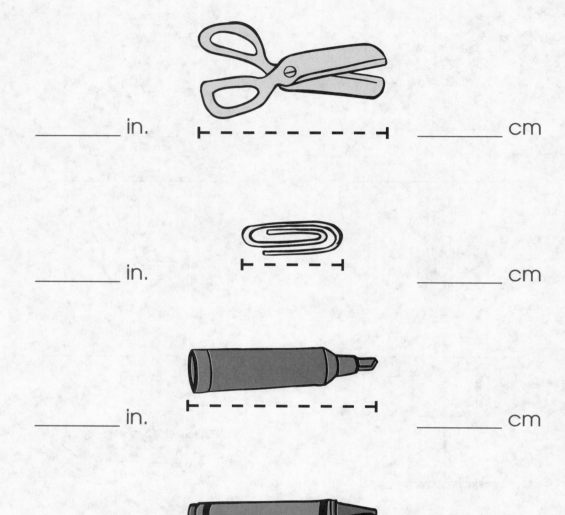

_____ in.   _____ cm

_____ in.   _____ cm

_____ in.   _____ cm

_____ in.   _____ cm

_____ in.   _____ cm

Inches & Centimeters

Measure the length of each paintbrush to the nearest inch. Measure it again to the nearest centimeter. In each pair, circle the longer paintbrush.

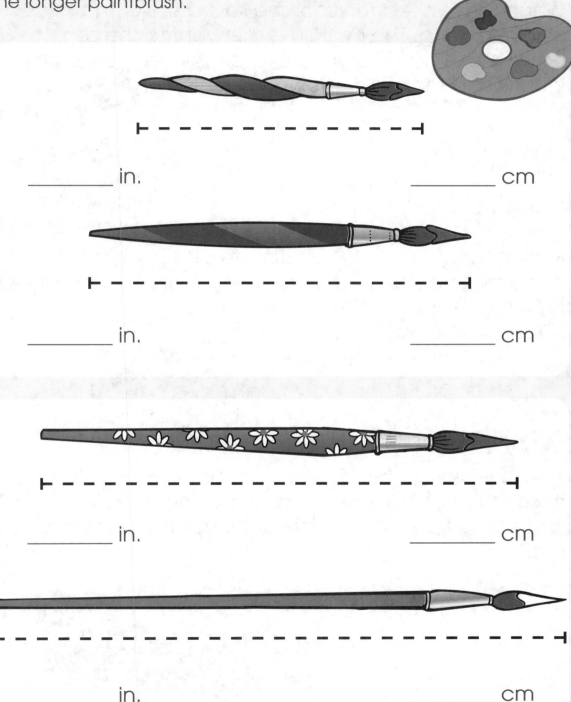

_____ in.   _____ cm

_____ in.   _____ cm

_____ in.   _____ cm

_____ in.   _____ cm

Word Problems About Length

Read and solve.

When Riley visited the zoo, she saw a snake that was 35 inches long. The next time she went to the zoo, the same snake had grown to 57 inches long. How many inches had the snake grown?

_____ in.

Mateo's ribbon was 60 centimeters long. He cut 37 centimeters to use for wrapping a gift for his mother. How much ribbon did he have left?

_____ cm

A baby alligator measured 15 inches from the tip of its nose to its front legs. It measured 22 inches from its front legs to the tip of its tail. How long was the baby alligator in all?

_____ in.

Word Problems About Length

Read and solve.

Brock walked 33 meters from the swings to the monkey bars. He walked 27 meters from the monkey bars to the slide. How many meters did Brock walk in all?

_____ m

The distance from home plate to the pitcher's mound is 60 feet. The distance from home plate to second base is 90 feet. How much closer is the pitcher's mound to home plate?

_____ ft.

Jonathan and Dory were going to the park. They ran 38 meters of the way. They walked 62 meters of the way. How many meters did they travel in all?

_____ m

Number Lines

Use each number line to add. Make a mark on the number line at the first number. Count forward to add the second number. Make a mark on the sum. Write the sum.

37 + 6 = _____

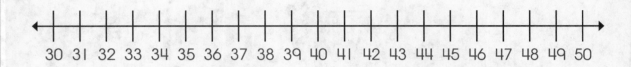

30 31 32 33 34 35 36 37 38 39 40 41 42 43 44 45 46 47 48 49 50

40 + 11 = _____

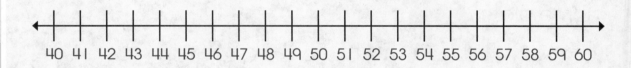

40 41 42 43 44 45 46 47 48 49 50 51 52 53 54 55 56 57 58 59 60

23 + 3 = _____

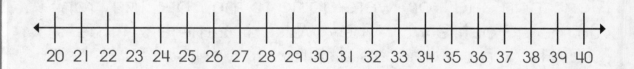

20 21 22 23 24 25 26 27 28 29 30 31 32 33 34 35 36 37 38 39 40

29 + 12 = _____

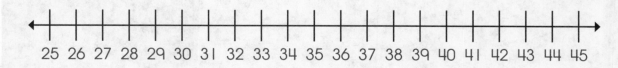

25 26 27 28 29 30 31 32 33 34 35 36 37 38 39 40 41 42 43 44 45

Number Lines

Create a number line to help solve each problem. Begin each number line with the number shown.

$25 + 6 =$ _____

25

$65 + 8 =$ _____

65

$77 + 5 =$ _____

77

Number Lines

Use each number line to subtract. Make a mark on the number line at the first number. Count backward to subtract the second number. Make a mark on the difference. Write the difference.

14 − 5 = _____

20 − 12 = _____

68 − 15 = _____

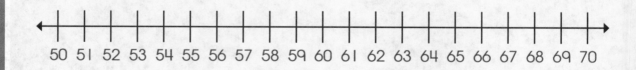

34 − 6 = _____

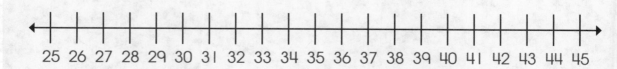

Number Lines

Create a number line to help solve each problem. Begin each number line with the number shown.

42 − 10 = _____

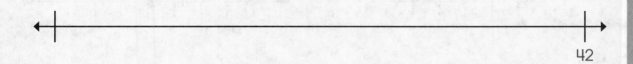

42

87 − 7 = _____

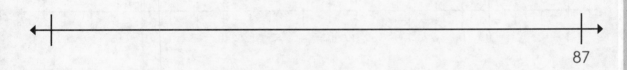

87

20 − 4 = _____

20

Number Lines

Read and solve. Show your work on the number line.

There were 150 students in the cafeteria. After eating lunch, 13 students went to the library. How many students did not go to the library?

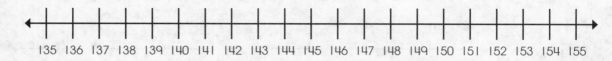

135 136 137 138 139 140 141 142 143 144 145 146 147 148 149 150 151 152 153 154 155

_____ students

11 children were playing together at the park. Then, 8 more children came to play. How many children were at the park playing together?

1 2 3 4 5 6 7 8 9 10 11 12 13 14 15 16 17 18 19 20 21

_____ children

At 10:00 in the morning, the temperature was 63 degrees. At noon, the temperature was 15 degrees higher. What was the temperature at noon?

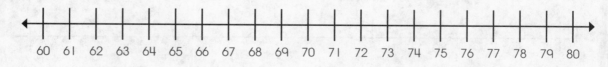

60 61 62 63 64 65 66 67 68 69 70 71 72 73 74 75 76 77 78 79 80

_____ degrees

Number Lines

Read and solve. Show your work on the number line.

Kyla had 95 coins. She gave 20 coins to Shonda. How many coins did Kyla have left?

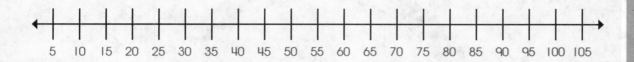

_____ coins

When Josie visited the aquarium, she saw 30 jellyfish, 40 crabs, and 50 turtles. How many animals did she see in all?

_____ animals

For a food drive, the first grade classes collected 200 items. The second grade classes collected 300 items. The third grade classes collected 100 items. How many items were collected in all?

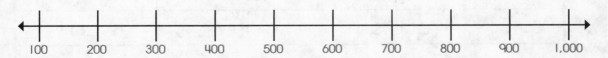

_____ items

Tell Time

Each time the long hand moves to a new number on the clock face, five minutes go by. There are 60 minutes in one hour. Count by fives to write the missing numbers around the clock.

Do a **time** challenge! How many times can you do each exercise in one minute? Use a kitchen timer or stopwatch app to time yourself. Write numbers to complete the chart.

Fitness Challenge	How Many Times in One Minute?
jumping jacks	
squats	
push-ups	
toe touches	

Health & Fitness

Tell Time

Circle the clock that shows each time.

2:45

9:55

4:30

12:25

223

Tell Time

Read each clock. Circle the time shown.

7:40

8:40

12:30

12:35

3:50

4:50

2:15

2:45

6:00

6:05

1:25

2:25

Tell Time

Match the clocks and times.

8:30

9:05

5:55

When you see someone being bullied, take it seriously. Do not let too much **time** pass before you act. Waiting will only make it worse. Instead, take these actions right away.

Look the bully in the eye. Say, "Stop it!"

Separate the bully and the person being bullied.

Tell a trusted adult.

Social Skills

Tell Time

Match the analog and digital clocks.

9:50

4:15

1:15

7:35

11:45

Tell Time

Read each clock. Write the time shown.

_____ : _____

_____ : _____

_____ : _____

_____ : _____

_____ : _____

_____ : _____

Tell Time

Read each clock. Write the time shown.

_____ : _____ _____ : _____

_____ : _____ _____ : _____

_____ : _____ _____ : _____

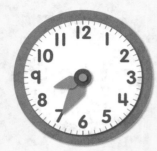

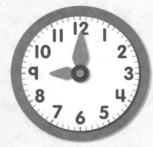

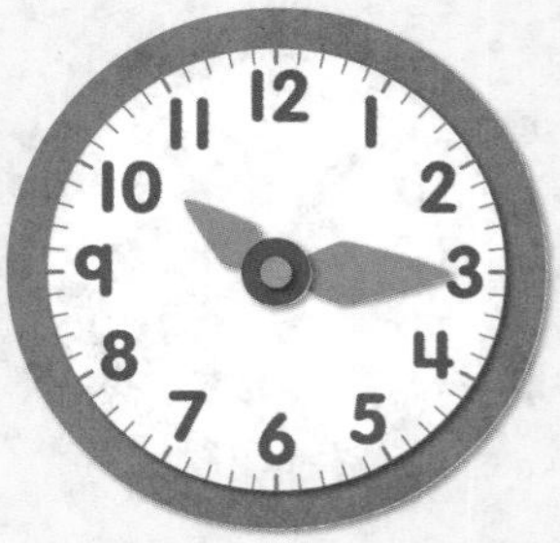

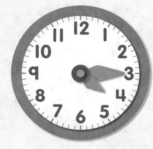

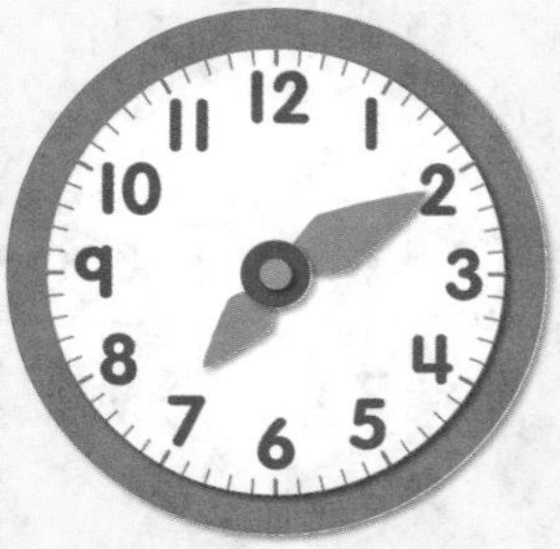

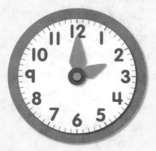

Tell Time

Draw hands on each clock to show the time.

1:20

8:30

12:40

6:15

9:45

10:00

Tell Time

Read the time on each digital clock. Draw hands on the analog clock to show the same time.

Tell Time

The 12 hours between 12:00 midnight and 12:00 noon are A.M. hours. The 12 hours between 12:00 noon and 12:00 midnight are P.M. hours. A.M. and P.M. stand for **ante meridiem** and **post meridiem**, ancient words that mean "before midday" and "after midday." Look at each picture and time. Write A.M. or P.M. to tell when the action is probably happening.

10:30 _____   7:45 _____

11:20 _____   8:15 _____

Draw a picture of what you might do at each **time** of day.

10:15 A.M.   **4:20 P.M.**   **7:30 P.M.**

All About Me

Tell Time

Match the times.

seven-thirty in the morning	12:00 A.M.
9:00 in the evening	a quarter 'til eleven o'clock at night
3:30 A.M.	9:00 P.M.
midnight	half-past three in the morning
10:45 P.M.	7:30 A.M.

Circle **A.M.** or **P.M.** for each event.

I like to watch the stars.   A.M.   P.M.

We watched the sunrise.   A.M.   P.M.

My brother naps in the afternoon.   A.M.   P.M.

We had a pancake breakfast.   A.M.   P.M.

Tell Time

Write the time shown on each clock. Then, circle **A.M.** or **P.M.**

Grace and Eddie play games during an afternoon thunderstorm. What time is it?

_____ : _____   **A.M.   P.M.**

Ms. Richardson says good morning to her students. What time is it?

_____ : _____   **A.M.   P.M.**

Vienna paints during her evening art class. What time is it?

_____ : _____   **A.M.   P.M.**

Buttons plays after his morning nap. What time is it?

_____ : _____   **A.M.   P.M.**

Count Money

Write the amount for each group of coins. Circle the group with the most cents.

penny 1¢

nickel 5¢

_____ ¢

_____ ¢

_____ ¢

_____ ¢

_____ ¢

_____ ¢

Count Money

Count the coins and write the total amount. Circle the group with the most cents.

penny 1¢

nickel 5¢

dime 10¢

_____ ¢

_____ ¢

_____ ¢

_____ ¢

_____ ¢

_____ ¢

Count Money

Match the groups of coins that are worth the same amount of money.

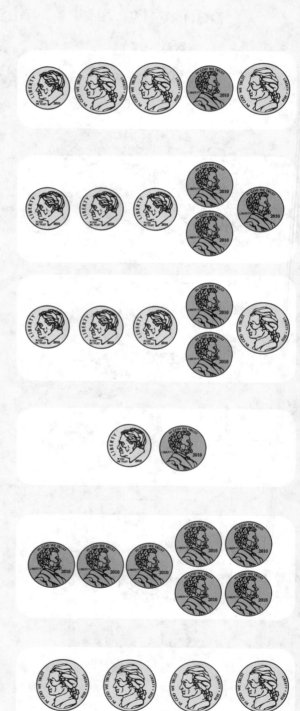

Count Money

Write the amount for each group of coins. Then, match each group of coins to a toy that costs the same amount.

   _____ ¢

31¢

    _____ ¢

47¢

 _____ ¢

16¢

 _____ ¢

36¢

 _____ ¢

23¢

Count Money

Write the amount for each group of coins. Circle the group of coins with the most cents.

penny 1¢   **nickel 5¢**   **dime 10¢**   **quarter 25¢**

_____ ¢

_____ ¢

_____ ¢

_____ ¢

_____ ¢

_____ ¢

Count Money

Match each amount to a group of coins.

Count Money

Money amounts less than 100 are worth less than one dollar. You can write these amounts with a dollar sign (**$**), **0** (to show that there are zero dollars), a decimal point (**.**), and the amount. Follow the examples. Circle the amount for each group of coins.

1¢ = $0.01   5¢ = $0.05   10¢ = $0.10   25¢ = $0.25

$0.15 $0.17 $0.12

$0.55 $0.57 $0.50

$0.29 $0.35 $0.39

$0.20 $0.25 $0.35

Make a kindness cup! Each time members of your family are kind to each other, put a small amount of **money** in the cup. It could be $0.10, $0.25, or $1.00. When the cup is full, use the money to buy a treat or pay for a family activity.

Count Money

One dollar is worth 100 cents. It is written **$1.00**. Count the bills in each group. Write the amount.

1 dollar = 100¢ = $1.00

$_____.00

$_____.00

$_____.00

$_____.00

$_____.00

$_____.00

Count Money

Write the amount for each group. Write the number of dollars before the decimal point (.). Write the number of cents after the decimal point (.). Circle the group worth the greatest amount.

$0.01	$0.05	$0.10	$0.25	$1.00

$_____._____

$_____._____

$_____._____

$_____._____

$_____._____

$_____._____

Count Money

Draw dollar bills and coins to show the amounts.

 $1.56

$0.87

$3.15

$1.40

$2.99

Count Money

Write the amount of money that answers each question.

$0.01 **$0.05** **$0.10** **$0.25** **$1.00**

I have one dollar, three quarters, one dime, and two pennies. How much money do I have?

$_____._____

You owe one quarter, one dime, and three pennies. How much money do you owe?

$_____._____

I paid three dollars, four dimes, and one nickel. How much money did I pay?

$_____._____

I have five dollars, five quarters, and five pennies. How much money do I have?

$_____._____

This costs two dollars, two quarters, two nickels, and two pennies. How much money does this cost?

$_____._____

I owe three dollars, four dimes, and two nickels. How much money do I owe?

$_____._____

Count Money

Compare the amount of money with the price of each item.
Is there enough money to buy the item? Circle **Yes** or **No**.

Yes   No

Yes   No

Yes   No

Yes   No

Money Word Problems

Read and solve. Use the pictures to help you.

Bryce bought a ball. He had one cent left. How much money did he have before buying the ball?

$_____ . _____ _____

Tara has 75¢. She buys a toy car. How much money does she have left?

$_____ . _____ _____

Jacob has 95¢. He buys a car and a ball. How much more money does he need to buy a doll for his cousin?

$_____ . _____ _____

Money Word Problems

Read and solve.

At the farmers market, squash are 3 for $1.25. Aidan bought 6 squash. He paid with 3 dollar bills. How much change did he get back?

$_____ . _____ _____

For 12 ears of corn, Mr. Jones paid 2 dollar bills, 2 quarters, 1 dime, and 1 nickel. How much did he pay for 12 ears of corn?

$_____ . _____ _____

Heads of lettuce cost $0.75 each. Rebecca wants to buy 3 heads of lettuce. She has $2.50. Does she have enough money? Circle your answer.

Yes   **No**

If the answer is yes, how much change will Rebecca get back?

$_____ . _____ _____

Line Plots

Ms. Lacey made a line plot to show the heights of the students in her second grade class. Use the line plot to answer the questions.

Heights of Ms. Lacey's Students (in.)

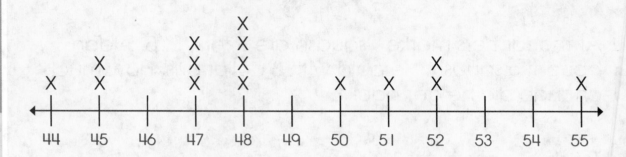

How many students are 47 inches tall?

_____ students

How many more students are 52 inches tall than 51 inches tall?

_____ student

Which group has more students? Circle your answer.

48 inches tall or less   49 inches tall or greater

How many students are less than 46 inches tall?

_____students

How many students did Ms. Lacey measure in all?

_____ students

Line Plots

During one afternoon outside, Devin found eight creatures and measured their lengths. Make a line plot to show Devin's data. Draw an **X** above the line plot for each creature.

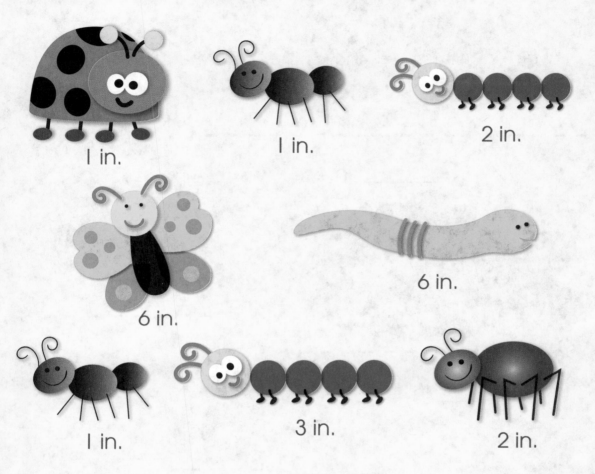

Length of Creatures Found in Devin's Backyard (in.)

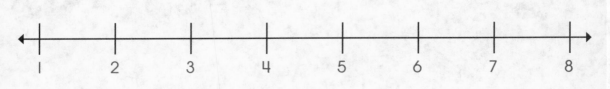

249

Line Plots

Use a ruler to measure each fish to the nearest inch.

_____ in.

_____ in.

_____ in.

_____ in.

_____ in.

_____ in.

_____ in.

_____ in.

Line Plots

Use the data you collected on page 250 to make a line plot. For each fish, draw an **X** above the line to show its measurement. Then, answer the questions.

Length of Fish (in.)

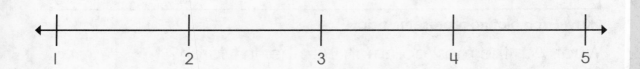

$$1 \qquad 2 \qquad 3 \qquad 4 \qquad 5$$

How many fish are 2 inches long?

 fish

How many more fish are 1 inch long than 3 inches long?

 fish

How many fish are 2 inches long or longer?

_____ fish

How many fish did you measure in all?

 fish

Picture Graphs

A picture graph uses pictures to represent numbers. Charley tracked the weather each day in the month of March. He made a picture graph to show his data. Use the graph to answer the questions.

Weather in March	
Sunny	☀ ☀ ☀ ☀ ☀ ☀ ☀ ☀ ☀ ☀
Cloudy	☁ ☁ ☁ ☁ ☁ ☁ ☁ ☁ ☁ ☁ ☁ ☁ ☁ ☁
Rainy	💧 💧 💧 💧 💧 💧
Snowy	❄ ❄

Key: Each picture represents 1 day.

What was the most common weather in March?
Circle your answer.

sunny   cloudy   rainy   snowy

What was the least common weather in March?
Circle your answer.

sunny   cloudy   rainy   snowy

Inventor Thomas Edison said, "Our greatest weakness lies in giving up. The most certain way to succeed is always to try just one more time." Look at the **picture graph**. Write the number of failures it shows before success.

Invention Results
💡 💡 💡 💡 💡 💡

Key: 💡 = failure   💡 = success

The chart shows _____ failures before one success.

Picture Graphs

Cady owns a cupcake shop. She made a picture graph to show how many cupcakes she sold each day for a week. Use the graph to answer the questions. Notice that each picture in the graph stands for more than one cupcake.

Cady's Cupcake Sales in One Week	
Monday	🧁🧁🧁🧁🧁🧁🧁🧁🧁🧁
Tuesday	🧁🧁🧁🧁
Wednesday	
Thursday	🧁🧁🧁🧁🧁🧁🧁🧁
Friday	🧁🧁🧁🧁🧁🧁🧁🧁🧁🧁🧁🧁

Key: 🧁 = 5 cupcakes

On Wednesday, Cady sold 15 cupcakes. Draw this data in the graph.

On which day did Cady sell the most cupcakes?

_____

How many cupcakes did Cady sell on Monday?

_____ cupcakes

How many more cupcakes did Cady sell on Thursday

than on Tuesday? _____ cupcakes

How many cupcakes did Cady sell this week?

_____ cupcakes

Picture Graphs

Count the treats sold at a movie theater during one hour.

Picture Graphs

Use the data you collected on page 254 to complete the picture graph. Notice that each picture you draw should stand for two treats sold. Use your graph to answer the questions.

Movie Theater Treats Sold in One Hour	
🍿	
🥤	
🥨	
🍬	

Key: Each picture represents 2 treats.

How many sodas were sold? _____ sodas

How many pretzels were sold? _____ pretzels

Did the movie theater sell more pretzels or more candy? Circle your answer.

candy   **pretzels**

Did the movie theater sell more soda or more candy? Circle your answer.

soda   **candy**

How many treats were sold in all? _____ treats

Bar Graphs

A bar graph uses bars of different lengths to show numbers. The students in Mr. Jamison's second grade class voted for their favorite desserts. They made a bar graph to show the data. Use the graph to answer the questions.

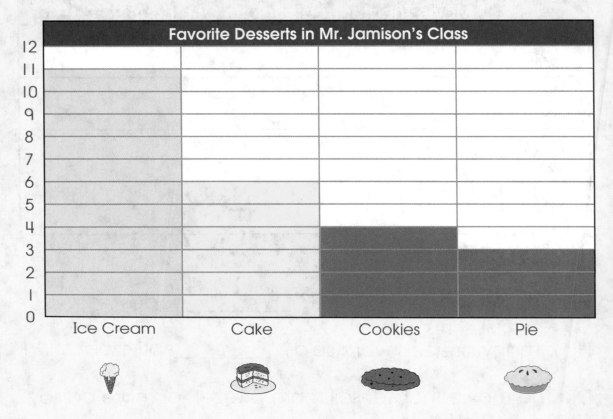

What is the class's favorite dessert? Circle your answer.

cake   **ice cream**   **cookies**   **pie**

What is the class's least favorite dessert? Circle your answer.

cake   **ice cream**   **cookies**   **pie**

How many more students chose cake than cookies?

_____ students

Bar Graphs

The students in room 22 made a chart to show how they get to school each morning. Use the data to complete the bar graph. Then, use your graph to answer the questions.

Form of Transportation	Number of Students
Walk	7
Bike	4
Car	10
Bus	8

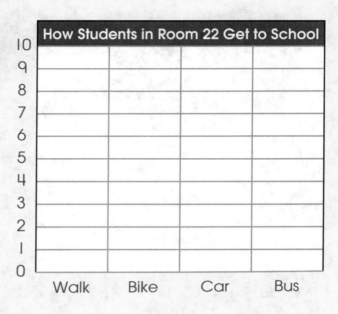

How many students walk or ride a bike to school?

_____ students

How many students ride in a car or bus to get to school?

_____ students

Later in the year, room 22 got a new student who walks to school. Now, how many students walk to school?

_____ students

How do you get to school? Add your information to the graph.

Bar Graphs

Count the items available for sale at Giuseppe's Fruit Stand.

Bar Graphs

Use the data you collected on page 258 to complete the bar graph. Then, use your graph to answer the questions.

Fruit at Giuseppe's Fruit Stand

10			
9			
8			
7			
6			
5			
4			
3			
2			
1			
0			
Watermelons	Pears	Lemons	Peaches

How many watermelons and lemons are for sale?

_____ watermelons and lemons

How many more pears are for sale than lemons?

_____ pears

How many pieces of fruit does Giuseppe have in all?

_____ pieces of fruit

Classify Flat Shapes

Count the sides and angles (corners) for each flat shape. Use the chart to help you write its name.

How many sides does it have?	3	4	5	6
How many angles does it have?	3	4	5	6
It is a…	triangle.	quadrilateral.	pentagon.	hexagon.

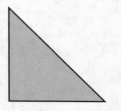  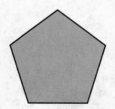

_____ _____ _____

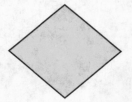 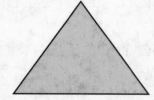 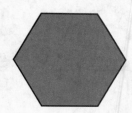

_____ _____ _____

 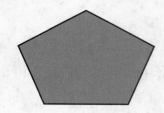 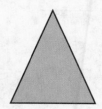

_____ _____ _____

Quadrilaterals

Any flat shape that has four sides and four angles is a quadrilateral. Color the quadrilaterals. Then, complete the sentences by writing the names of special quadrilaterals.

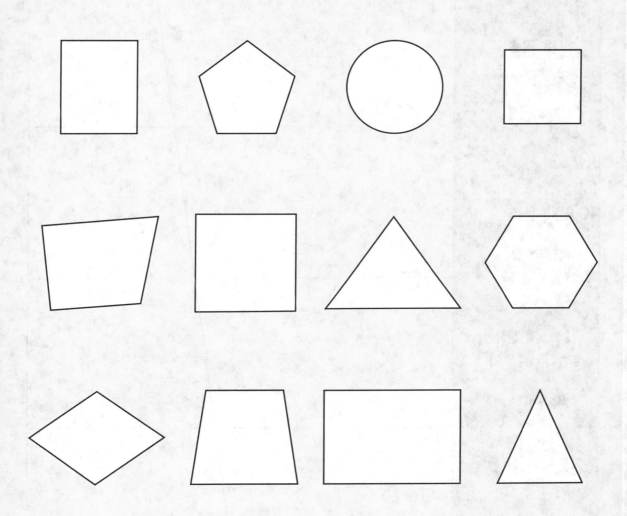

A quadrilateral with four equal sides and four right angles is a _____.

A quadrilateral with opposite sides of equal length and four right angles is a _____.

Shapes

Draw two different flat shapes to match each description.

It has 3 sides and 3 angles.	
It has 5 sides and 5 angles.	
It has 4 sides and 4 angles.	
It has 8 sides and 8 angles.	
It has 6 sides and 6 angles.	

Classify Solid Shapes

Solid shapes are three-dimensional. They have faces that are flat shapes, edges where the faces meet, and vertices (corners) where the edges meet. Cut out the solid shapes. Tape or glue them in the spaces to match their descriptions.

It has no faces, no edges, and no vertices.

It has 6 faces that are squares. It has 12 edges and 8 vertices.

It has 1 rectangular face and 4 triangular faces. It has 8 edges and 5 vertices.

It has 6 faces that are quadrilaterals. It has 12 edges and 8 vertices.

BLANK PAGE FOR CUTTING ACTIVITY

Draw Solid Shapes

Trace each solid shape.

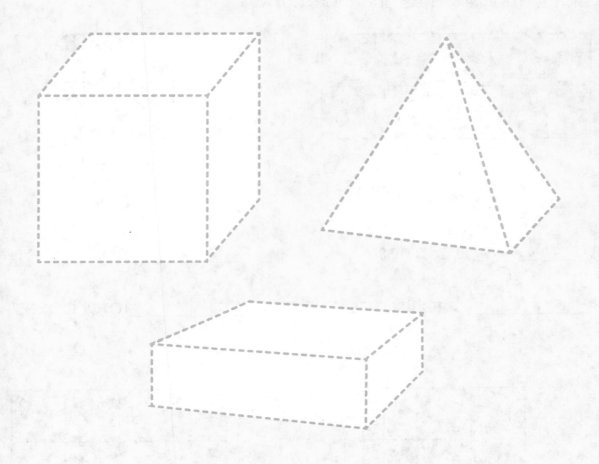

Find a **solid** cube. It could be a toy block or a block of wood purchased from a craft store. On each face, use a permanent marker to write the name of something you are grateful for. It could be a person, an animal, something you own, something you can do, or an opportunity you have. When you feel sad or jealous, roll the cube. Focus on feeling grateful for what is written on the face that comes up.

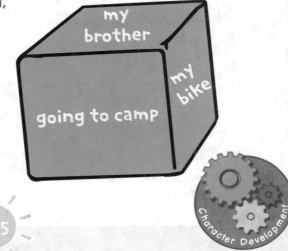

265

Character Development

Partition Shapes

Count the rows, columns, and total number of boxes in each shape. The first one is done for you.

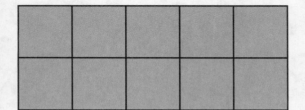

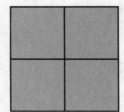

__2__ rows

__5__ columns

__10__ total boxes

_____ rows

_____ columns

_____ total boxes

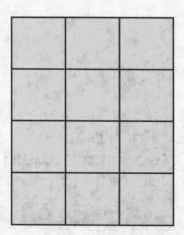

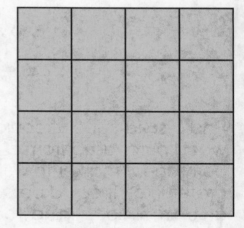

_____ rows

_____ columns

_____ total boxes

_____ rows

_____ columns

_____ total boxes

Partition Shapes

Count the rows, columns, and total number of boxes in each shape.

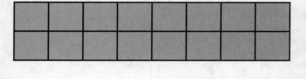

_____ rows

_____ columns

_____ total boxes

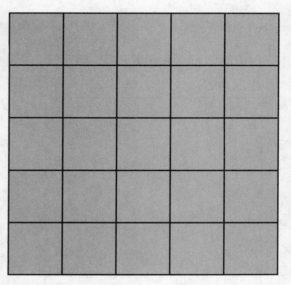

_____ rows

_____ columns

_____ total boxes

Partition the shape below into six boxes. In each box, write a way you help your family with household chores. Think of ways you help in the kitchen, bathroom, bedroom, and outside. If you did not fill all the boxes, think of more ways that you could help.

Partition Shapes

Follow the directions to divide each shape. Write how many same-sized units (boxes) you created.

Make 3 columns and 3 rows.

_____ same-sized units

Make 4 columns and 2 rows.

_____ same-sized units

Make 2 columns and 3 rows.

_____ same-sized units

Make 5 columns and 4 rows.

_____ same-sized units

Partition Shapes

Read each problem. Color same-sized units to help you find the answer.

Amelia and her mother are making a quilt for a new baby cousin. The quilt will have 5 rows and 6 columns of squares. How many quilt squares will Amelia and her mother need?

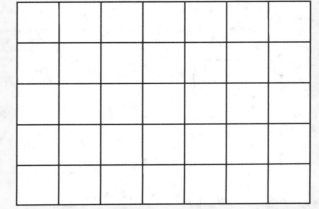

They will need _____ quilt squares.

Nick and his dad made a pan of brownies for an after-school snack. Nick wants to divide the brownies into 3 rows and 4 columns. How many same-sized brownies will Nick make?

Nick will make _____ same-sized brownies.

Halves

A half is one part of a whole that is divided into two equal shares. Color the shapes that are divided into halves, or two equal parts.

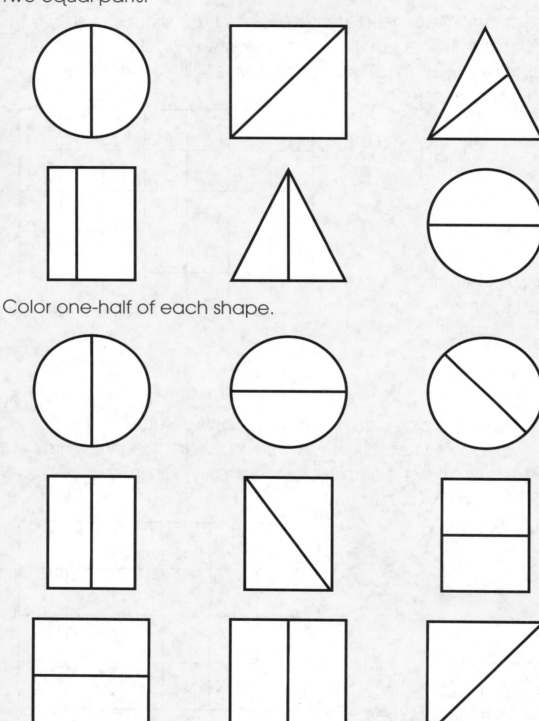

Color one-half of each shape.

Fourths

A fourth, or a quarter, is one part of a whole that is divided into four equal shares. Color the shapes that are divided into fourths, or four equal parts.

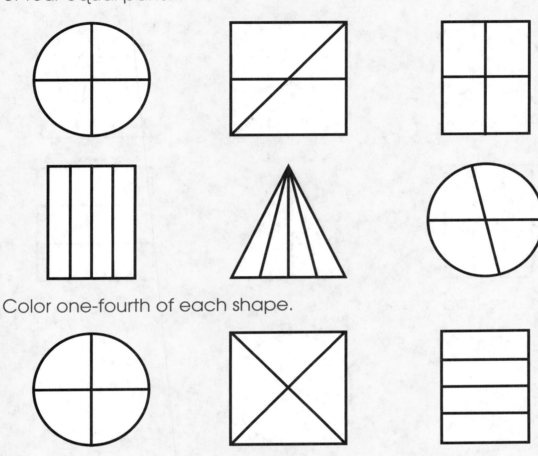

Color one-fourth of each shape.

A healthy meal includes vegetables, fruits, whole grains (such as brown rice and whole wheat noodles), and protein (such as lean meats and nuts). Draw a favorite food in each **fourth** of the dinner plate.

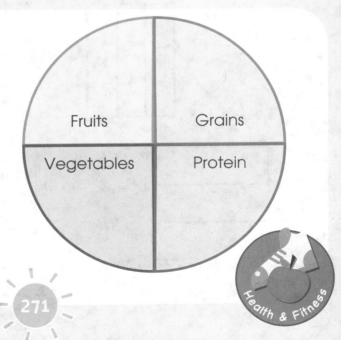

Fruits Grains

Vegetables Protein

Health & Fitness

Thirds

A third is one part of a whole that is divided into three equal shares. Color the shapes that are divided into thirds, or three equal parts.

Color one-third of each shape.

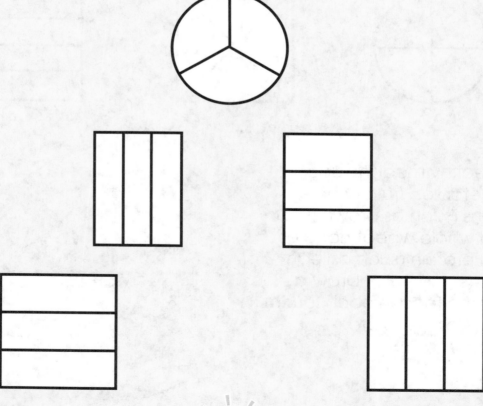

Equal Shares

Each shape is divided into equal shares. Circle the word that tells what part is shaded.

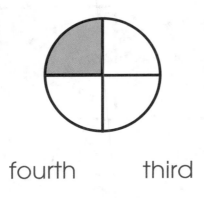

fourth   third

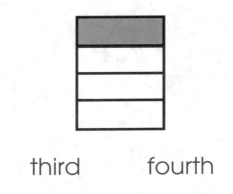

third   fourth

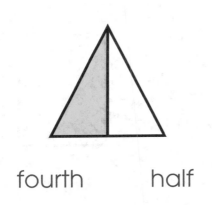

fourth   half

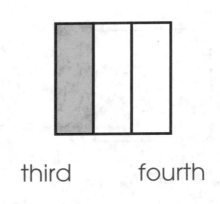

third   fourth

half   third

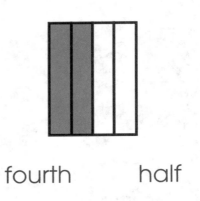

fourth   half

273

Equal Shares

Divide each shape into equal shares.

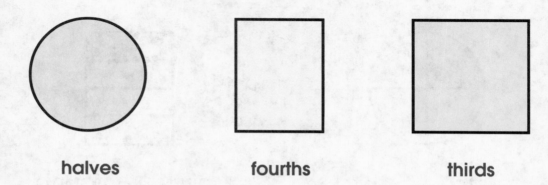

| halves | fourths | thirds |

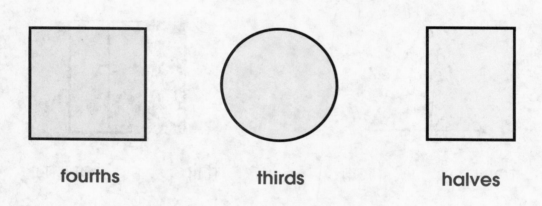

| fourths | thirds | halves |

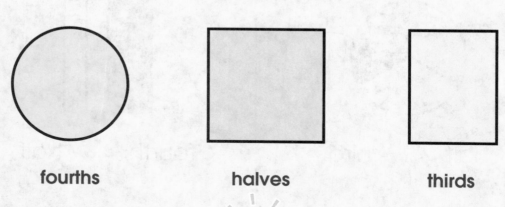

| fourths | halves | thirds |

Equal Shares & Wholes

Color the number of equal parts shown for each shape. Notice that one whole is the same as two halves, three thirds, or four fourths.

I fourth

2 fourths

3 fourths

4 fourths = I whole

I third

2 thirds

3 thirds = I whole

I half

2 halves = I whole

Answer Key

6

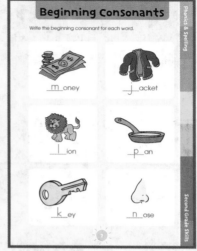

7

8

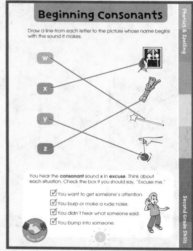

9

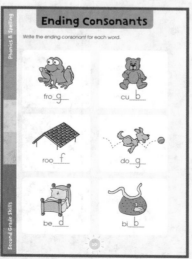

10

11

Answer Key

12

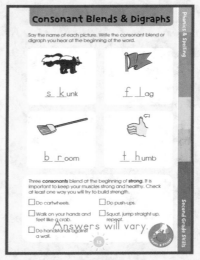

13

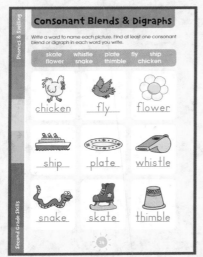

14

15

16

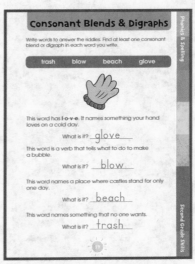

17

Double Consonants

To spell some words, double the consonant in the middle of the word. Write words to match the pictures and complete the puzzles. In each word you write, double the consonant shown.

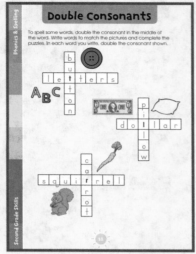

18

Double Consonants

To spell some words, double the consonant in the middle of the word. Write words to match the pictures and complete the puzzles. In each word you write, double the consonant shown.

There is a **double consonant** in **hobby**. Circle something that represents a hobby you enjoy or draw something on your own.

Answers will vary.

19

Silent Consonants

Some words have consonants that you cannot hear at all, such as **gh** in **night**, **w** in **wrong**, and **l** in **walk**. Write a word to name each picture. Underline at least one silent consonant in each word you write.

wrench   comb   eight   lamb   wrist   calf

wrist   eight

calf   lamb

wrench   comb

20

Silent Consonants

Write a word to name each picture. Underline at least one silent consonant in each word you write.

knee   thumb   light   knife   whistle   knob

knife   whistle

thumb   light

knee   knob

21

Hard & Soft c

When **c** is followed by **e**, **i**, or **y**, it usually has a soft sound, like the **c** in **pencil**. When **c** is followed by **a**, **o**, or **u**, it usually has a hard sound, like the **c** in **cat**. Say each word. If it has a soft **c** sound, write it under the pencil. If it has a hard **c** sound, write it under the cat.

| dance | carrot | cent | card |
| popcorn | cookie | mice | rice |

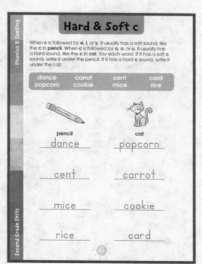

pencil → dance

cat → popcorn

cent   carrot

mice   cookie

rice   card

22

Hard & Soft g

When **g** is followed by **e**, **i**, or **y**, it usually has a soft sound, like the **g** in **giraffe**. When **g** is followed by **a**, **o**, or **u**, it usually has a hard sound, like the **g** in **gate**. Say each word. If it has a soft **g** sound, write it under the giraffe. If it has a hard **g** sound, write it under the gate.

| engine | garden | cage | magic |
| giant | goes | gum | goal |

giraffe → engine

gate → garden

giant   goes

cage   gum

magic   goal

23

Answer Key

Short Vowels

Say the name of each picture. Complete the word by writing the letter that spells the short vowel sound.

n_e_t s_o_ck l_i_ps

b_o_ttle p_u_p l_a_dder

h_a_t p_e_nny p_i_n

24

Short Vowels

Say the name of each picture. Complete the word by writing the letter that spells the short vowel sound.

a_x p_o_pcorn t_e_nt

th_i_mble b_u_tton f_o_x

h_a_mmer p_u_ppet c_a_ndle

25

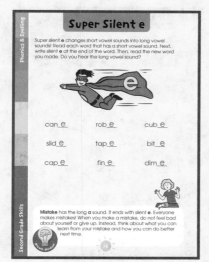

Super Silent e

Super silent e changes short vowel sounds into long vowel sounds! Read each word that has a short vowel sound. Next, write silent e at the end of the word. Then, read the new word you made. Do you hear the long vowel sound?

can_e_ rob_e_ cub_e_

slid_e_ tap_e_ bit_e_

cap_e_ fin_e_ dim_e_

Mistake has the long **a** sound. It ends with silent **e**. Everyone makes mistakes! When you make a mistake, do not feel bad about yourself or give up. Instead, think about what you can learn from your mistake and how you can do better next time.

26

Vowel Teams

Long vowel sounds are often spelled by two vowels together, or vowel teams. Unscramble and write each word. Circle the vowel team.

s_e_e_d f_e_e_t

p_a_i_l s_e_a_t

g_o_a_t s_a_i_l

27

Vowel Teams

In words with vowel teams, the first vowel letter often says its name, or makes a long vowel sound. The second vowel letter is silent. Read each long vowel word. Circle the vowel that makes the long vowel sound. Draw a box around the vowel that is silent.

t e a r   b o a t   p e a s

m e a t   c o a t   r a i n

The long **a** sound in **wait** is spelled with the vowel team **ai**. When you have something to say, it can be hard to wait for your turn to talk. Check one way you will try to not interrupt.

Answers will vary.

☐ Be interested in what others say. Make sure you understand their ideas.

☐ Patiently raise your hand or use another signal to show that you have something to say.

☐ In a group, pass around a toy or another object. When someone is holding the toy, everyone else must listen. Make sure everyone has a turn.

28

Long a Spellings

Read each word. Write it under the letters that spell the long **a** sound.

| eight | plain | maze | basic | way |
| apron | sunray | waited | brave | weigh |

a
apron basic

a-consonant-silent e
brave maze

ay
way sunray

ai
waited plain

ei
eight weigh

29

Answer key

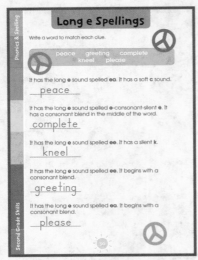

Long e Spellings

Write a word to match each clue.

peace   greeting   complete
kneel   please

It has the long e sound spelled ea. It has a soft c sound.

peace

It has the long e sound spelled e-consonant-silent e. It has a consonant blend in the middle of the word.

complete

It has the long e sound spelled ee. It has a silent k.

kneel

It has the long e sound spelled ee. It begins with a consonant blend.

greeting

It has the long e sound spelled ea. It begins with a consonant blend.

please

30

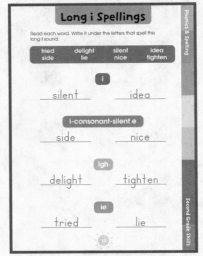

Long i Spellings

Read each word. Write it under the letters that spell the long i sound.

tried   delight   silent   idea
side   lie   nice   tighten

i

silent   idea

i-consonant-silent e

side   nice

igh

delight   tighten

ie

tried   lie

31

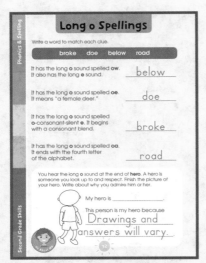

Long o Spellings

Write a word to match each clue.

broke   doe   below   road

It has the long o sound spelled ow. It also has the long e sound.

below

It has the long o sound spelled oe. It means "a female deer."

doe

It has the long o sound spelled o-consonant-silent e. It begins with a consonant blend.

broke

It has the long o sound spelled oa. It ends with the fourth letter of the alphabet.

road

You hear the long o sound at the end of hero. A hero is someone you look up to and respect. Finish the picture of your hero. Write about why you admire him or her.

My hero is _____

This person is my hero because
Drawings and answers will vary.

32

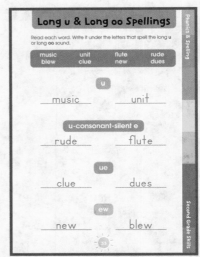

Long u & Long oo Spellings

Read each word. Write it under the letters that spell the long u or long oo sound.

music   unit   flute   rude
blew   clue   new   dues

u

music   unit

u-consonant-silent e

rude   flute

ue

clue   dues

ew

new   blew

33

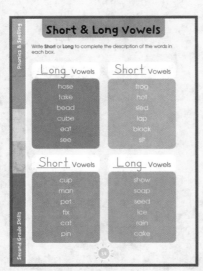

Short & Long Vowels

Write **Short** or **Long** to complete the description of the words in each box.

Long Vowels
hose
take
bead
cube
eat
see

Short Vowels
frog
hot
sled
lap
block
sit

Short Vowels
cup
man
pet
fix
cat
pin

Long Vowels
show
soap
seed
ice
rain
cake

34

Short & Long Vowels

Write the missing letters. Then, decide whether each word has a short vowel sound or a long vowel sound. Circle your choice.

(long) short	long (short)	long (short)
k i te	a pe	l o ck
(long) short	long (short)	(long) short
h o s e	tr u ck	v a s e
(long) short	long (short)	long (short)
l i ght	p e ach	l i ps

35

Answer Key

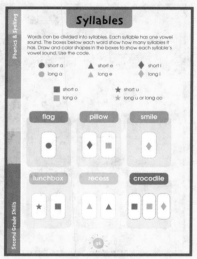

36

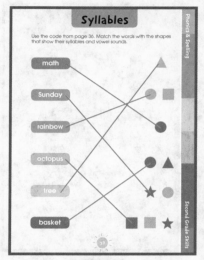

37

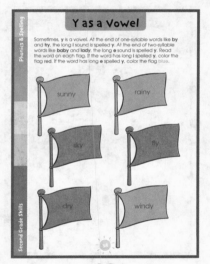

38

39

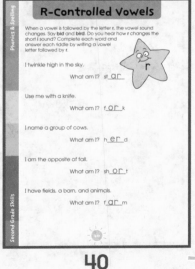

40

41

Special Vowel Teams

The vowel teams **ou** and **ow** can spell the same vowel sound. You hear it in **cloud** and **clown**. Write **ou** or **ow** to complete each word.

o_ow_l   c_ou_ch

h_ou_se   t_ow_el

p_ow_der   m_ou_se

m_ou_th   h_ow_l

42

Special Vowel Teams

The vowel teams **oy** and **oi** can spell the same vowel sound. You hear it in **joy** and **foil**. Write **oy** or **oi** to complete each word.

b_oi_l   t_oy_s

b_oy_   c_oi_n

The vowel teams **au** and **aw** can spell the same vowel sound. You hear it in **because** and **low**. Write **au** or **aw** to complete each word.

_au_to   s_aw_

p_aw_   s_au_ce

43

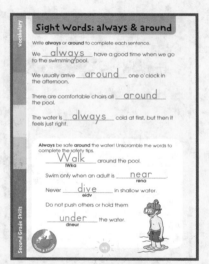

Sight Words: always & around

Write **always** or **around** to complete each sentence.

We ___always___ have a good time when we go to the swimming pool.

We usually arrive ___around___ one o'clock in the afternoon.

There are comfortable chairs all ___around___ the pool.

The water is ___always___ cold at first, but then it feels just right.

Always be safe **around** the water! Unscramble the words to complete the safety tips.

___Walk___ around the pool.
lWka

Swim only when an adult is ___near___
rena

Never ___dive___ in shallow water.
eidv

Do not push others or hold them
___under___ the water.
dneur

44

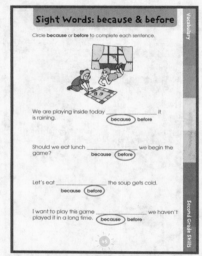

Sight Words: because & before

Circle **because** or **before** to complete each sentence.

We are playing inside today _____ it is raining.   (because) before

Should we eat lunch _____ we begin the game?   because (before)

Let's eat _____ the soup gets cold.   because (before)

I want to play this game _____ we haven't played it in a long time.   (because) before

45

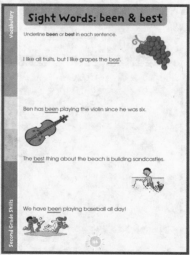

Sight Words: been & best

Underline **been** or **best** in each sentence.

I like all fruits, but I like grapes the best.

Ben has been playing the violin since he was six.

The best thing about the beach is building sandcastles.

We have been playing baseball all day!

46

Sight Words: does & don't

Write **does** or **don't** to complete each sentence. Do not forget to put the apostrophe (') in the correct place each time you write **don't**.

Can you run as fast as Erin ___does___ ?

I ___don't___ think so, but I can try!

___Don't___ you want to play fetch, Baxter?

I bet Smokey ___does___! Let's go find him.

Write **does** or **don't** to complete each sentence about good friends.

A good friend ___does___ listen to you.

Good friends ___don't___ brag and try to "one up" each other.

Good friends ___don't___ say mean things about you.

A good friend ___does___ stick by you in good times and bad.

47

Sight Words: fast & first

Find and circle **fast** and **first** in the puzzle. Each word appears six times. Look across and down. Circle **fast** in green. Circle **first** in blue.

```
e f f i r s t w e w s
d u f l k o g c i f t
s i a h j f r x c b f
f a s t e r t f l r i
i e t o w i s a f i r
r d t u r j k s a l s
s s y i f i r t s a t
t f i r s t u i t e f
b n l m p l o u e v a
s a f i r s t w a t s
f s t s r n f i r s t
f a s t d w u y i l b
```

48

Sight Words: gave & goes

Circle the socks with **gave**.

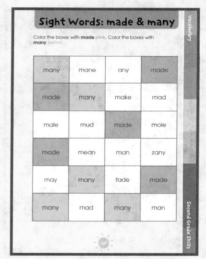

Circle the socks with **goes**.

Circle **gave** or **goes** in each sentence.

That sock goes in this drawer.

My mom gave me money for doing chores.

49

Sight Word: its

The word **its** is a possessive. It shows that something is owned by something else. Do not confuse the word with **it's**, which means "it is." Read the story. Circle **its** each time it appears.

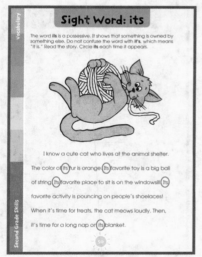

I know a cute cat who lives at the animal shelter.
The color of its fur is orange. Its favorite toy is a big ball
of string. Its favorite place to sit is on the windowsill. Its
favorite activity is pouncing on people's shoelaces!
When it's time for treats, the cat meows loudly. Then,
it's time for a long nap on its blanket.

50

Sight Words: made & many

Color the boxes with **made** pink. Color the boxes with **many** yellow.

many	mane	any	made
made	many	make	mad
male	mud	made	mole
made	mean	man	zany
may	many	fade	made
many	mad	many	man

51

Sight Words: off & or

Write **off** or **or** to complete each sentence.

We could stay home, __or__ we could go to the soccer game.

The wind blew the leaves __off__ the trees.

Would you rather build a snowman __or__ go sledding?

My umbrella kept the rain __off__ my head.

52

Sight Words: pull & read

Write **pull** or **read** to complete each sentence.

Donna must __pull__ the weeds before she plants flowers.

Mrs. Higgins and Adam __read__ to the class.

Juan uses the wagon to __pull__ his toys.

Ryder found a book to __read__ on the trip.

53

Answer Key

Sight Words: right & sing

Circle the balloons with **right**.

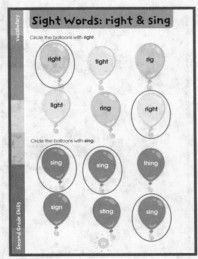

Circle the balloons with **sing**.

Sight Words: tell & their

The word **their** is used to show that something is owned. Do not confuse it with **there**, which names a place, or with **they're**, which means "they are." Circle **their** in each sentence.

The students went over there to sharpen their pencils.

They're bringing their famous chili to the party.

Circle **tell** in each box.

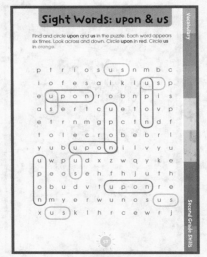

Call 9-1-1 only in a real emergency. Call if someone is seriously injured, if you see signs of fire, or if someone is in danger. When you call, be ready to **tell**:

• What the emergency is.
• Where you are. (If you don't know the address, tell what roads or places are nearby.)
• What phone number you are calling from.
• Who is hurt or in need of rescue.

9-1-1

54   **55**

Sight Words: these & those

Underline **these** and **those** in the sentences.

What will grow from these seeds?

Are these rain boots yours?

Those boys are cheering loudly.

Those flowers smell so good!

I saw those cookies at the store, but I like these better.

I washed all of these dishes, but those will have to wait.

Sight Words: upon & us

Find and circle **upon** and **us** in the puzzle. Each word appears six times. Look across and down. Circle **upon** in red. Circle **us** in orange.

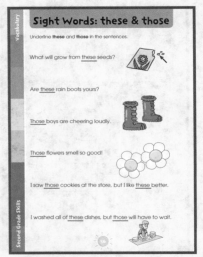
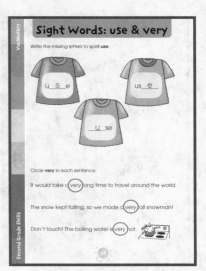

56   **57**

Sight Words: use & very

Write the missing letters to spell **use**.

u _ s e
us _ e
_ u _ se

Circle **very** in each sentence.

It would take a very long time to travel around the world.

The snow kept falling, so we made a very tall snowman!

Don't touch! The boiling water is very hot.

Sight Words: which & why

Circle **which** or **why** to complete each sentence.

Which / Why   do you prefer, the green shirt or the purple one?

Which / Why   did you choose to play baseball?

Which / Why   is Mrs. Posy wearing a bandage?

I don't know   which / why   way to go.

What do you dream of doing someday? Complete the title. Then, write to explain **why** you want to make your dream come true.

Why I Want to _____

Answers will vary.

58   **59**

Answer Key

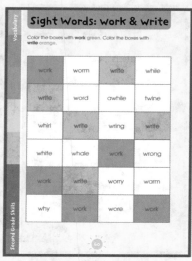

Sight Words: work & write

Color the boxes with **work** green. Color the boxes with **write** orange.

work	worm	write	while
write	word	awhile	twine
whirl	write	wring	write
white	whale	work	wrong
work	write	worry	warm
why	work	wore	work

60

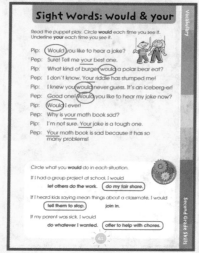

Sight Words: would & your

Read the puppet play. Circle **would** each time you see it. Underline **your** each time you see it.

Pip: (Would) you like to hear a joke?
Pep: Sure! Tell me your best one.
Pip: What kind of burger (would) a polar bear eat?
Pep: I don't know. Your riddle has stumped me!
Pip: I knew you (would) never guess. It's an iceberg-er!
Pep: Good one! (Would) you like to hear my joke now?
Pip: (Would) I ever!
Pep: Why is your math book sad?
Pip: I'm not sure. Your joke is a tough one.
Pep: Your math book is sad because it has so many problems!

Circle what you **would** do in each situation.

If I had a group project at school, I would
left others do the work.   (do my fair share.)

If I heard kids saying mean things about a classmate, I would
(tell them to stop.)   join in.

If my parent was sick, I would
do whatever I wanted.   (offer to help with chores.)

61

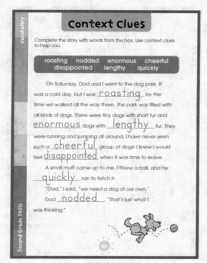

Context Clues

Complete the story with words from the box. Use context clues to help you.

roasting   nodded   enormous   cheerful
disappointed   lengthy   quickly

On Saturday, Dad and I went to the dog park. It was a cold day, but I was __roasting__ by the time we walked all the way there. The park was filled with all kinds of dogs. There were tiny dogs with short fur and __enormous__ dogs with __lengthy__ fur. They were running and jumping all around. I have never seen such a __cheerful__ group of dogs! I knew I would feel __disappointed__ when it was time to leave.

A small mutt came up to me. I threw a ball, and he __quickly__ ran to fetch it.

"Dad," I said, "we need a dog of our own."

Dad __nodded__. "That's just what I was thinking."

62

Context Clues

Complete the story with words from the box. Use context clues to help you.

fluffy   sample   savory   gobble
raw   nibbled   bare

One sunny day, my whole family had a picnic at the park. My grandmother prepared __savory__ chicken. Grandpa baked some __fluffy__ rolls. My uncle brought __raw__ vegetables and dip. My mom made something green and white in a big dish. I ate the chicken, two rolls, and some vegetables. I liked it all! Then, my brother looked in the dish our mom had brought.

"Did you try it?" I asked him.

"You're my big brother," he said. "You __sample__ it!"

I __nibbled__ a tiny bit. It was good! But the dish was almost __bare__. "It's terrible!" I told my brother. "I'll eat the rest of it so you won't have to."

My brother watched me __gobble__ it all up. I tried not to look too happy!

63

Classifying

Write a word from the box to tell what could be described by each group of words.

soup   puppy   storm   ocean   book
dishes   winter   kite   car

sand	snow	string
shells	wind	tail
waves	cold	wind
fish	ice	fly
__ocean__	__winter__	__kite__

rain	soft	broth
thunder	furry	carrots
wind	playful	tomatoes
hail	small	noodles
__storm__	__puppy__	__soup__

cup	pages	tires
plate	words	seats
bowl	pictures	window
platter	cover	trunk
__dishes__	__book__	__car__

64

Classifying

Draw an **X** on the word in each row that does not belong.

apple pie	~~peas~~	pudding	ice cream
green beans	cucumbers	corn	~~bread~~
peaches	oranges	~~cream~~	apples
cheese	milk	~~rice~~	yogurt
napkin	spoon	~~salad~~	knife

Healthy snacks provide energy to help you work, play, and learn. Look at the **classified** healthy snacks. Write one more in each category.

Fruits
apple
raisins

Vegetables
celery sticks
cherry tomatoes

__Answers will vary.__

Grains
granola bar
wheat crackers

Dairy
cheese stick
chocolate milk

65

285

Answer key

Prefixes

Change the meaning of each sentence by adding the prefix to the **bold** word.

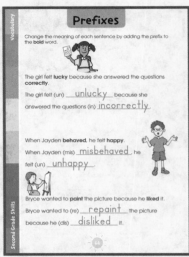

The girl felt **lucky** because she answered the questions **correctly**.

The girl felt (un) __unlucky__ because she answered the questions (in) __incorrectly__.

When Jayden **behaved**, he felt **happy**.

When Jayden (mis) __misbehaved__, he felt (un) __unhappy__

Bryce wanted to **paint** the picture because he **liked** it.

Bryce wanted to (re) __repaint__ the picture because he (dis) __disliked__ it.

66

Suffixes

Add the suffixes to the base words. Write the new words and use them to complete the sentences below.

help + ing = __helping__   talk + ed = __talked__
care + less = __careless__   love + ly = __lovely__
build + er = __builder__   loud + er = __louder__

My mother __talked__ to my teacher about the field trip.

The radio was __louder__ than the television.

Those flowers are __lovely__ !

Madison was being __careless__ when she lost the permission slip.

Marshall thinks he is the best __builder__ when it comes to blocks.

Kyle is __helping__ to fold the laundry.

67

Base Words

Look at the first word in each row. Circle its base word.

starring	(star)	starred
looking	looked	(look)
recycle	(cycle)	cycling
preview	(view)	viewing
unfriendly	friendly	(friend)
happier	unhappy	(happy)

Underline the **base word** shared by each pair of words. Then, circle the word in each pair that best describes you.

helpful / unhelpful   disrespectful / respectful   friendly / unfriendly   flexible / inflexible

68

Word Parts

Look at each word. Write its prefix, base word, and suffix in the chart. Not all words have all three parts. You may need to change the spelling of the base word. The first one is done for you.

	Prefix	Base Word	Suffix
tallest		tall	est
unhappy	un	happy	
recycling	re	cycle	ing
unfairly	un	fair	ly
informal	in	formal	
distrusted	dis	trust	ed
thankful		thank	ful
underground	under	ground	
younger		young	er
misspoke	mis	spoke	
rewritten	re	write	en
incorrectly	in	correct	ly

69

Shades of Meaning

Look at each group of words. Which word has the strongest meaning? Use it to complete the sentence.

fell   crashed   tumbled
The glass plate __crashed__ to the ground.

plunges   hops   leaps
The frog __plunges__ into the pond.

devoured   ate   nibbled
The boy quickly __devoured__ his breakfast.

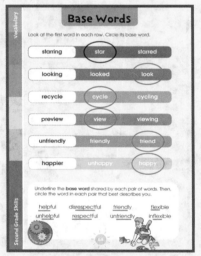

Write a stronger word for the **bold** word in each sentence. Possible answers shown.
"Hello, Mrs. Carter," Hannah **said**. __exclaimed__

The children **walk** out the door when the bell rings. __rush__

Ahmed and I really **like** this movie. __adore__

70

Shades of Meaning

Look at each group of words. Which word has the strongest meaning? Use it to complete the sentence.

angry   cross   furious
Tonio was __furious__ with his brother.

tasty   delicious   yummy
My dad cooked a __delicious__ dinner tonight.

pretty   nice   stunning
The flowers in your garden are __stunning__ !

Write a stronger word for the **bold** word in each sentence. Possible answers shown.
The **hungry** cat sat near its empty bowl. __starving__

Playing basketball is **fun**. __exciting__

The movie we watched last night was **bad**. __horrible__

71

Answer key

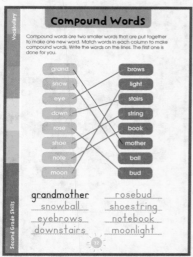

Compound Words

Compound words are two smaller words that are put together to make one new word. Match words in each column to make compound words. Write the words on the lines. The first one is done for you.

grand	brows
snow	light
eye	stairs
down	string
rose	book
shoe	mother
note	ball
moon	bud

grandmother   rosebud
snowball   shoestring
eyebrows   notebook
downstairs   moonlight

72

Compound Words

Combine two words from the box to make a compound word that names each picture. You may use the words more than once.

box   room   hall   rain   sand   melon
way   bed   water   lunch   coat

sandbox   raincoat
watermelon   lunchbox
hallway   bedroom

Playing a sport is a good way to stay fit and healthy. Combine each word with **ball** to make a **compound word** that names a sport. Circle your favorite sport to play.

volley ball   foot ball
kick ball   basket ball
base ball   soft ball

73

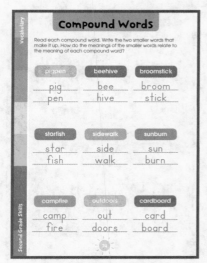

Compound Words

Read each compound word. Write the two smaller words that make it up. How do the meanings of the smaller words relate to the meaning of each compound word?

pigpen	beehive	broomstick
pig	bee	broom
pen	hive	stick

starfish	sidewalk	sunburn
star	side	sun
fish	walk	burn

campfire	outdoors	cardboard
camp	out	card
fire	doors	board

74

Compound Words

Combine the underlined words to make a compound word that answers each question.

What is a berry that is blue?   blueberry
What is the time to go to bed?   bedtime
What is a room for a class?   classroom
What is the top of a tree?   treetop
What is a case for a book?   bookcase
What is a place for a fire?   fireplace
What is a pan for a dish?   dishpan
What is a cloth for the table?   tablecloth

75

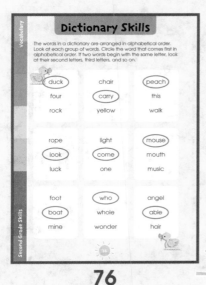

Dictionary Skills

The words in a dictionary are arranged in alphabetical order. Look at each group of words. Circle the word that comes first in alphabetical order. If two words begin with the same letter, look at their second letters, third letters, and so on.

(duck)	chair	(peach)
four	(carry)	this
rock	yellow	walk

rope	light	(mouse)
(look)	(come)	mouth
luck	one	music

foot	(who)	angel
(boat)	whole	(able)
mine	wonder	hair

76

Dictionary Skills

The guide words at the top of a dictionary page tell what the first and last words on that page will be. Only words that come in alphabetical order between those two words will be on that page. Write each word in alphabetical order between the guide words.

faint   fan   fence   farm   feed
family   farmer   face   far   feet

face	fence
face	farm
faint	farmer
family	feed
fan	feet
far	fence

77

Answer Key

Dictionary Skills

A picture dictionary contains words, word meanings, and pictures. Complete the picture dictionary page. Write the missing definitions.

Answers will vary. Possible answers shown.

baby
a very young child

band
a group of people that plays music

bank
a place where money is kept

bark
the sound a dog makes

berry
a small, juicy fruit

board
a flat piece of wood

78

Dictionary Skills

When words have more than one meaning, the meanings are numbered in a dictionary. Read the meanings for **tag**. Write the number of the correct definition after each sentence.

tag
1. a small strip or tab attached to something else
2. to label
3. to follow closely and constantly
4. a game of chase

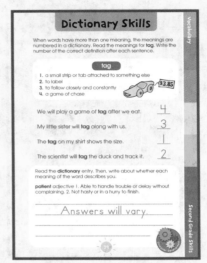

We will play a game of **tag** after we eat. — 4

My little sister will **tag** along with us. — 3

The **tag** on my shirt shows the size. — 1

The scientist will **tag** the duck and track it. — 2

Read the **dictionary** entry. Then, write about whether each meaning of the word describes you.

patient adjective 1. Able to handle trouble or delay without complaining. 2. Not hasty or in a hurry to finish.

Answers will vary.

79

Nouns

Decide whether each noun names a person, place, or thing. Write it under the correct category. Then, circle each common noun. Draw a box around each proper noun.

bridge   Elm Park   Malik Jones   cousin
park   Golden Gate Bridge

Person
Malik Jones   cousin

Place
Elm Park   park

Thing
bridge   Golden Gate Bridge

Look at each **common noun**. Write a matching **proper noun** that names someone who is special to you. Draw a picture of each person.

teacher   relative   friend

Drawings and answers will vary.

80

Collective Nouns

A collective noun names a group of people, animals, or things. Circle the collective noun in each phrase. Then, match it to the group it names.

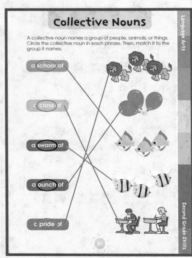

a **school** of

a **class** of

a **swarm** of

a **bunch** of

a **pride** of

81

Plurals

Write the plural of each noun. Add **s** or **es**. If the word ends in **y**, change **y** to **i** before adding **es**. If the word ends in **f** or **fe**, change **f** to **v** before adding **s** or **es**.

dog → penny

dogs   pennies

ax   class
axes   classes

peach   blueberry
peaches   blueberries

party   wife
parties   wives

boot   city
boots   cities

leaf   walrus
leaves   walruses

82

Irregular Plurals

The plurals of some nouns do not follow the rules you know. Look at the noun above each sentence. Write its irregular plural to finish the sentence.

feet   teeth   deer   children   women

tooth
I lost my two front __teeth__

woman
The __women__ in Mom's club are best friends.

foot
The clown had big __feet__

child
The __children__ played hide-and-seek.

deer
__Deer__ live in this forest.

83

Answer key

Pronouns

Rewrite each sentence using a pronoun to replace the noun in **bold**.

her	them	they	he	it

The owl has a nest in the old barn.

It has a nest in the old barn.

Give the books to **Ethan and Tara**.

Give the books to them.

Marcus watched the bird land.

He watched the bird land.

Everyone cheered for **Alice**.

Everyone cheered for her.

Georgia and Finn went to the zoo.

They went to the zoo.

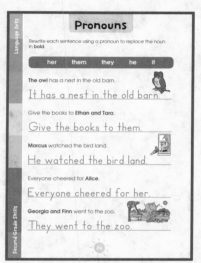

84

Reflexive Pronouns

Reflexive pronouns refer back to a noun in the sentence. They often end in **-self** or **-selves**. Write a reflexive pronoun to complete each sentence.

myself	ourselves	herself	itself
	himself	yourselves	

My little sister likes to dress   herself

"Behave yourselves ," said the teacher to her students.

I taught   myself   how to roller skate.

My brother drove   himself   to school today.

We entertained ourselves by playing with cars.

Maya's dog ran away, but it came back home by   itself   .

85

Verbs

Underline the verb in each sentence about spiders. The verb tells what spiders do or what spiders are.

A spider <u>is</u> an arachnid.

Spiders <u>spin</u> webs of silk.

They <u>wait</u> in the center of their webs.

Then, they <u>sink</u> their fangs into trapped insects.

Female spiders <u>wrap</u> silk around their eggs for protection.

Most spiders <u>are</u> harmless to people.

Do spiders <u>scare</u> you?

Write a **verb** to complete each sentence.

I can   Answers will vary.

I can _____

I can't _____ yet, but I will keep trying and getting better!

86

Verb Tenses

Write **past**, **present**, or **future** to tell the tense of the verb in each sentence.

It will rain tomorrow. future

Tomas is singing a song. present

He played lacrosse. past

I will buy a sandwich. future

Molly is sleeping. present

Dad worked hard today. past

Find the verb in each sentence. Rewrite it in the tense shown.

Mia played with her new friend. (present) plays

Hasaan is calling him. (future) will call

Holly and Luisa walk here. (past) walked

87

Irregular Verbs

Some past-tense verbs do not follow the rules you know. They do not end in **ed**. Rewrite each sentence in the past tense. Use an irregular verb.

blew	gave	grew	took	came

I will grow another inch this year.

I grew another inch this year.

I will blow out the candles.

I blew out the candles.

Everyone will give me presents.

Everyone gave me presents.

All my cousins will come.

All my cousins came.

The party will take three hours.

The party took three hours.

88

Irregular Verbs

Circle the irregular verb that completes each sentence.

Scientists have (find/(found)) the cure.

The coach (speaks/(spoke)) to us yesterday.

The teacher (rings/(rang)) the bell earlier.

She (says/(said)) it twice already.

Grace (sings/(sang)) in the school concert last year.

89

Answer Key / Second Grade Skills

Irregular Verbs

Write verbs to complete the chart.

Present Tense	Past Tense	Future Tense
It _goes_	It went	It will go
She has	She _had_	She will have
He _sees_	He saw	He will see
It eats	It ate	It _will eat_
She leaves	She _left_	She will leave
He makes	He made	He _will make_
It flies	It _flew_	It will fly
She _wears_	She wore	She will wear

90

Irregular Verbs

Use past-tense verbs from the chart on page 90 to complete the sentences.

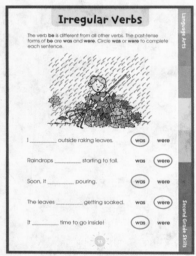

The plane _flew_ high above the clouds.

We _ate_ cranberries for Thanksgiving last year.

Cinnamon _made_ that bread taste so good.

Last weekend, we _went_ camping in our favorite spot by the lake.

Grandpa already _left_ to go to the store.

We _had_ a great time at the party.

My sister _wore_ a dragon costume for Halloween.

She _saw_ a raccoon under the bridge.

91

Irregular Verbs

The verb **be** is different from all other verbs. The present-tense forms of **be** are **am**, **is**, and **are**. Write **am**, **is**, or **are** to complete each sentence.

My friends _are_ helping me build a tree house.

It _is_ in my backyard.

We _are_ using hammers, wood, and nails.

It _is_ a very hard job.

I _am_ lucky to have such good friends.

92

Irregular Verbs

The verb **be** is different from all other verbs. The past-tense forms of **be** are **was** and **were**. Circle **was** or **were** to complete each sentence.

I _____ outside raking leaves. (was) / were

Raindrops _____ starting to fall. was / (were)

Soon, it _____ pouring. (was) / were

The leaves _____ getting soaked. was / (were)

It _____ time to go inside! (was) / were

93

Adjectives

Adjectives describe nouns. They answer questions like these: What kind? How many? How much? Write two adjectives from the story that describe each **bold** noun.

Super Soup

On a cold winter **morning**, my mom said, "Let's make soup. It will be ready for lunch." We made a pot of hot vegetable **soup**. First, I put sweet white **onions** in the pot. Then, I added three cleaned **carrots**. Next into the pot were ripe, juicy **tomatoes**. Last, we added crisp, fresh **potatoes**. The soup cooked for a long time. Finally, we ate our super soup for lunch as snowflakes swirled outside. It was the best soup I ever had!

morning	onions	carrots
cold	sweet	three
winter	white	cleaned

tomatoes	potatoes	soup
ripe	crisp	hot
juicy	fresh	vegetable

Read **adjectives** from **a** to **z**. Circle those that describe you!

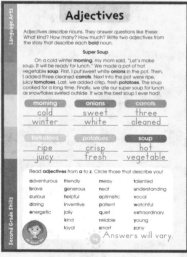

adventurous	friendly	messy	talented
brave	generous	neat	understanding
curious	helpful	optimistic	vocal
daring	inventive	patient	watchful
energetic	jolly	quiet	extraordinary
	kind	reliable	young
	loyal	smart	zany

Answers will vary.

94

Adverbs

Adverbs describe verbs. They often end in **ly**. They answer questions like these: Where? How? When? Circle the adverb in each sentence. Write the adverb to answer the question.

The doctor listened (carefully).

How did the doctor listen? _carefully_

The call was returned (yesterday).

When was the call returned? _yesterday_

She lost her shoes (somewhere).

Where did she lose her shoes? _somewhere_

He did the work (perfectly).

How did he do the work? _perfectly_

They (often) jump rope.

When do they jump rope? _often_

95

Answer key

Adjectives & Adverbs

Circle the adjective or adverb that describes the **bold** word and completes the sentence.

The sun **rose** _____ in the East.

quick · (quickly)

Vera kicked the _____ **ball** into the air.

(bouncy) · bouncily

Paul _____ **peeked** around the corner.

slow · (slowly)

Corey did not study and got a _____ **grade**.

(bad) · badly

Sari's _____ **project** won first prize.

(creative) · creatively

I thought _____ before I made my next **move**.

serious · (seriously)

96

Adjectives & Adverbs

Circle the adjective or adverb that completes each sentence. If you circle an adjective, underline the noun it describes. If you circle an adverb, underline the verb it describes.

The cat (quiet/(quietly)) slept under the table.

The ((brave)/bravely) police officer helped the boy.

The couple danced to the ((loud)/loudly) song.

My little brother (neat/(neatly)) made his bed.

Underline an **adjective** or an **adverb** in each bike safety rule.

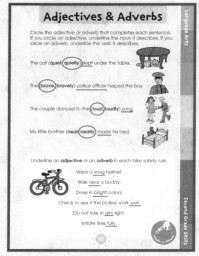

Wear a snug helmet.

Ride near a buddy.

Dress in bright colors.

Check to see if the brakes work well.

Do not ride in dim light.

Inflate tires fully.

97

Expand Sentences

Use the adjectives and adverbs shown to expand and rewrite each sentence.

swiftly · old

Parker ran down the dirt path.

Parker ran swiftly down the old dirt path.

loyal · dearly

Seth loves his dog.

Seth dearly loves his loyal dog.

always · pink

Ana wears glasses.

Ana always wears pink glasses.

colorful · everywhere

Before the party, Mom hung banners.

Before the party, Mom hung colorful banners everywhere.

98

Expand Sentences

Add adjectives, adverbs, and other words to expand the sentences and provide more information.

The friends chatted.

Answers will vary.

Their team lost the game.

Squirrels chased each other.

His phone buzzed.

The storm raged.

99

Simple Sentences

A simple sentence has one noun/verb pair. The noun part of the sentence is the subject. The verb part of the sentence is the predicate. Circle the noun in each simple sentence. Underline the verb in each simple sentence. Draw a line between the subject and the predicate. The first one is done for you.

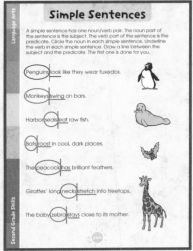

(Penguins) look like they wear tuxedos.

(Monkeys) swing on bars.

Harbor (seals) eat raw fish.

(Bats) roost in cool, dark places.

The (peacock) has brilliant feathers.

Giraffes' long (necks) stretch into treetops.

The baby (zebra) stays close to its mother.

100

Simple Sentences

When the subject (noun part) of a sentence has two nouns, it is a compound subject. When the predicate (verb part) of a sentence has two verbs, it is a compound predicate. Combine each pair of sentences into one simple sentence with a compound subject, compound predicate, or both. You will need to add the word **and**. The first one is done for you.

The gymnast grabbed the bar. The gymnast flipped.

The gymnast grabbed the bar and flipped.

Roses grow in the garden. Tulips grow in the garden.

Roses and tulips grow in the garden.

Dad chopped firewood. Dad stacked firewood.

Dad chopped and stacked firewood.

Coats keep us warm in winter. Sweaters keep us warm in winter.

Coats and sweaters keep us warm in winter.

Students choose books. Students read silently.

Students choose books and read silently.

101

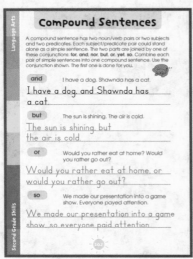

Compound Sentences

A compound sentence has two noun/verb pairs or two subjects and two predicates. Each subject/predicate pair could stand alone as a simple sentence. The two parts are joined by one of these conjunctions: for, and, nor, but, or, yet, so. Combine each pair of simple sentences into one compound sentence. Use the conjunction shown. The first one is done for you.

and — I have a dog. Shawnda has a cat.
I have a dog, and Shawnda has a cat.

but — The sun is shining. The air is cold.
The sun is shining, but the air is cold.

or — Would you rather eat at home? Would you rather go out?
Would you rather eat at home, or would you rather go out?

so — We made our presentation into a game show. Everyone payed attention.
We made our presentation into a game show, so everyone paid attention.

102

Compound Sentences

Write compound sentences. Choose one subject/predicate pair from the first box, a conjunction from the middle box, and one subject/predicate pair from the last box.

Libby could go to the festival. / Libby went to the festival. / Libby rode the roller coaster. / Libby played arcade games.

and / but / or

she rode the Ferris wheel. / she did not win any prizes. / she could stay home. / she did not stay long.

Answers will vary. Possible answers shown.

1. Libby could go to the festival, or she could stay home.
2. Libby went to the festival, but she did not stay long.
3. Libby rode the roller coaster, and she rode the Ferris wheel.
4. Libby played arcade games, but she did not win any prizes.

103

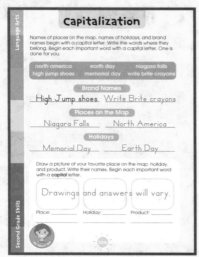

Capitalization

Names of places on the map, names of holidays, and brand names begin with a capital letter. Write the words where they belong. Begin each important word with a capital letter. One is done for you.

north america / earth day / niagara falls / high jump shoes / memorial day / write brite crayons

Brand Names
High Jump shoes — Write Brite crayons

Places on the Map
Niagara Falls — North America

Holidays
Memorial Day — Earth Day

Draw a picture of your favorite place on the map, holiday, and product. Write their names. Begin each important word with a **capital** letter.

Drawings and answers will vary.

Place: _____ Holiday: _____ Product: _____

104

Commas

Follow the directions to write a letter to a family member or friend.

Letters will vary.

Write the month, the day, a comma (,), and the year.

Write a greeting that begins with **Dear**. Then, write the person's name. Write a comma (,) after the person's name.

Write a friendly message.

Write a closing. Some closings are: **Sincerely**, **Yours Truly**, or **Your Friend**. Write a comma (,) after the closing.

Sign your name on the line below the closing.

105

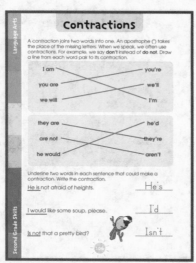

Contractions

A contraction joins two words into one. An apostrophe (') takes the place of the missing letters. When we speak, we often use contractions. For example, we say **don't** instead of **do not**. Draw a line from each word pair to its contraction.

I am — I'm
you are — you're
we will — we'll

they are — they're
are not — aren't
he would — he'd

Underline two words in each sentence that could make a contraction. Write the contraction.

<u>He is</u> not afraid of heights. — He's

<u>I would</u> like some soup, please. — I'd

<u>Is not</u> that a pretty bird? — Isn't

106

Contractions

Write the two words that make up each contraction.

we've __we__ + __have__   I'm __I__ + __am__
she's __she__ + __is__   you'll __you__ + __will__
can't __can__ + __not__   haven't __have__ + __not__

Write the words as contractions.

you have __you've__   I am __I'm__
they are __they're__   he will __he'll__
it will __it'll__   they had __they'd__
had not __hadn't__   is not __isn't__

Having a growth mindset means believing that hard work will help you learn, grow, and reach your goals. Look at the chart to see how to change limiting thoughts into thoughts that show a growth mindset. Circle a **contraction** in each sentence.

Instead of …	Try thinking…
(I'm) not good at this.	I'm going to keep getting better.
(I'd) better just give up.	I'll try a different way.
(I'll) never be that smart.	I'm getting smarter all the time.

107

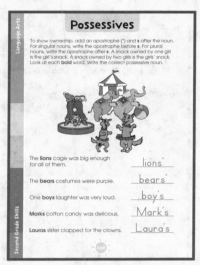

Possessives

To show ownership, add an apostrophe (') and **s** after the noun. For singular nouns, write the apostrophe before **s**. For plural nouns, write the apostrophe after **s**. A snack owned by one girl is the girl's snack. A snack owned by two girls is the girls' snack. Look at each **bold** word. Write the correct possessive noun.

The **lions** cage was big enough for all of them. — lions'

The **bears** costumes were purple. — bears'

One **boys** laughter was very loud. — boy's

Marks cotton candy was delicious. — Mark's

Lauras sister clapped for the clowns. — Laura's

108

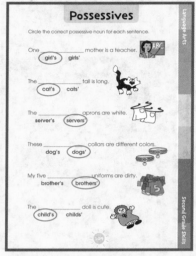

Possessives

Circle the correct possessive noun for each sentence.

One (girl's) mother is a teacher.

The (cat's) tail is long.

The server's (servers') aprons are white.

These dog's (dogs') collars are different colors.

My five brother's (brothers') uniforms are dirty.

The (child's) doll is cute.

109

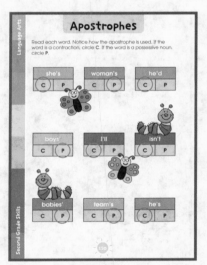

Apostrophes

Read each word. Notice how the apostrophe is used. If the word is a contraction, circle **C**. If the word is a possessive noun, circle **P**.

she's — (C) P
woman's — C (P)
he'd — (C) P

boys' — C (P)
I'll — (C) P
isn't — (C) P

babies' — C (P)
team's — C (P)
he's — (C) P

110

Apostrophes

Circle the contractions and possessive nouns that are written correctly. Write the other words correctly under the category where they belong.

mans'	I'l	wouldve'
(weren't)	(we'll)	sh'es
ca'nt	(Victor's)	(I've)
(baby's)	womans'	wolfs'
childs'	(you're)	(wolves)

Contractions
can't
I'll
would've
she's

Possessives
man's
child's
woman's
wolf's

111

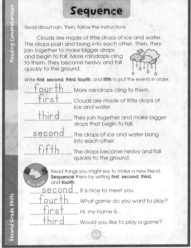

Sequence

Read about rain. Then, follow the instructions.

Clouds are made of little drops of ice and water. The drops push and bang into each other. Then, they join together to make bigger drops and begin to fall. More raindrops cling to them. They become heavy and fall quickly to the ground.

Write **first**, **second**, **third**, **fourth**, and **fifth** to put the events in order.

fourth — More raindrops cling to them.
first — Clouds are made of little drops of ice and water.
third — They join together and make bigger drops that begin to fall.
second — The drops of ice and water bang into each other.
fifth — The drops become heavy and fall quickly to the ground.

Read things you might say to make a new friend. **Sequence** them by writing **first**, **second**, **third**, and **fourth**.

second — It is nice to meet you.
fourth — What game do you want to play?
first — Hi, my name is...
third — Would you like to play a game?

112

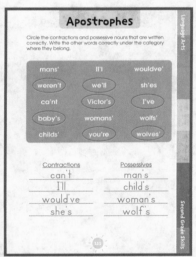

Sequence

Read the story. Then, follow the instructions.

One Saturday morning in May, Olivia and Anna went to the zoo. First, they bought tickets to get into the zoo. Second, they visited the Gorilla Garden and had fun watching the gorillas stare at them. Then, they went to Tiger Town and watched the tigers as they slept in the sunshine. Fourth, they went to Hippo Haven and laughed at the hippos cooling off in their pool. Next, the girls visited Snake Station and learned about poisonous and nonpoisonous snakes. It was noon, and they were hungry, so they ate lunch at Parrot Patio.

Write **first**, **second**, **third**, **fourth**, **fifth**, and **sixth** to put the events in order.

fourth — They went to Hippo Haven.
first — Olivia and Anna bought zoo tickets.
third — They watched the tigers sleep.
sixth — They ate lunch at Parrot Patio.
second — The gorillas stared at them.
fifth — They learned about snakes.

113

293

114

Classify

Use a red crayon to circle the names of three animals that would make good pets. Use a blue crayon to circle the names of three wild animals. Use an orange crayon to circle the two animals that live on a farm.

| bear | lion | bird | cow |
| cat | sheep | dog | tiger |

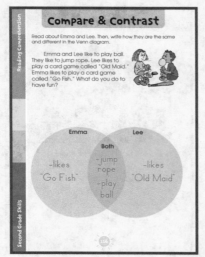

```
a m e o w w n l i o n
b m d o g x i l s o
a b e a r r v l m h r
r m r m o o u s e e k
k c a b b i r d s e m
i o t t i g e r m p q
b w n o w w r q n o n
d n c p h h i d u d n
f k c a t t r o a r m
```

115

Classify

Write words from the box where they belong.

bush	strawberries	apple juice
airplane	honey	grass
rocket	flower	bird

These things taste sweet.

strawberries   honey   apple juice

These things can fly.

airplane   rocket   bird

These things grow in the ground.

bush   flower   grass

People with a growth mindset believe that, through hard work, they can change, grow, and learn. **Classify** the thoughts. Draw a line from each one to **Fixed Mindset** or **Growth Mindset**.

- I can either do it, or I can't.
- There is no limit to how much I can learn.
- I stick to what I know.
- Challenges help me grow.

Growth Mindset
Fixed Mindset

116

Compare & Contrast

Read about Emma and Lee. Then, write how they are the same and different in the Venn diagram.

Emma and Lee like to play ball. They like to jump rope. Lee likes to play a card game called "Old Maid." Emma likes to play a card game called "Go Fish." What do you do to have fun?

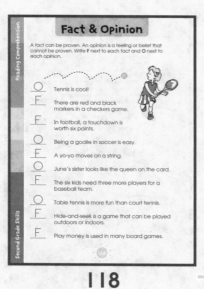

Emma — likes "Go Fish"
Both — jump rope, play ball
Lee — likes "Old Maid"

117

Compare & Contrast

Read about Marvin and Mugsy. Then, complete the Venn diagram, telling how they are the same and different.

Maggie has two dogs, Marvin and Mugsy. Marvin is a dalmatian. Marvin likes to run after balls in the backyard. His favorite food is Canine Crunchy Crunch. Maggie likes to take Marvin for walks. Then, Marvin loves to sleep in his doghouse. Mugsy is a big, furry brown dog. Since she is big, she needs lots of exercise. Maggie takes her for walks in the park. Her favorite food is Canine Crunchy Crunch. Mugsy likes to sleep on Maggie's bed.

Marvin — dalmatian, runs after balls, sleeps in his doghouse
Both — eat Canine Crunchy Crunch, go for walks
Mugsy — big furry brown dog, needs lots of exercise, sleeps on Maggie's bed

118

Fact & Opinion

A fact can be proven. An opinion is a feeling or belief that cannot be proven. Write F next to each fact and O next to each opinion.

O — Tennis is cool!

F — There are red and black markers in a checkers game.

F — In football, a touchdown is worth six points.

O — Being a goalie in soccer is easy.

F — A yo-yo moves on a string.

O — June's sister looks like the queen on the card.

F — The six kids need three more players for a baseball team.

O — Table tennis is more fun than court tennis.

F — Hide-and-seek is a game that can be played outdoors or indoors.

F — Play money is used in many board games.

119

Fact & Opinion

Read the story. Write F next to each fact and O next to each opinion.

My name is Henrietta, and I am a humpback whale. I live in cold seas in the summer and warm seas in the winter. My long flippers are used to move forward and backward. I like to eat fish. Sometimes, I show off by leaping out of the water. Would you like to be a humpback whale?

O — Being a humpback whale is fun.

F — Humpback whales live in cold seas during the summer.

O — Whales are fun to watch.

F — Humpback whales use their flippers to move forward and backward.

O — Henrietta is a great name for a whale.

O — Leaping out of water would be hard.

F — Humpback whales like to eat fish.

F — Humpback whales show off by leaping out of the water.

Answer key

Predict

Look at each picture. Draw and write what you predict will happen next.

Answers will vary.

Recognizing expressions on people's faces can help you **predict** how they are feeling. Then, you know better what to say and how to help. Draw a face to show each feeling.

proud   disappointed   angry   surprised

Drawings will vary.

120

Predict

Read the story. Then, answer the questions.

Maggie had a great idea for a game to play with her dogs Marvin and Mugsy. The game was called "Dog Derby." Maggie would stand at one end of the driveway and hold on to the dogs by their collars. Her friend Mitch would stand at the other end of the driveway. When he said, "Go!" Maggie would let go of the dogs and they would race to Mitch. The first one there would get a dog biscuit. If there was a tie, both dogs would get a biscuit.

Which dog do you think will win the race?

Why? ___Answers will vary.___

What do you think will happen when they race again?

121

Answer Questions

Read about snakes. Then, answer the questions.

There are many facts about snakes that might surprise people. A snake's skin is dry. Most snakes are shy. They will hide from people. Snakes eat mice and rats. They do not chew them up. Snakes' jaws drop open so they can swallow their food whole.

A snake's skin is ___dry___

Most snakes are ___shy___

Snakes eat ___mice___ and ___rats___.

How do snakes eat? ___Their jaws drop open so they can swallow their food whole.___

Did any facts about snakes surprise you? Which ones?
___Answers will vary.___

122

Answer Questions

Read about sharks. Then, answer the questions.

Angela learned a lot about sharks when her class visited the aquarium. She learned that sharks are fish. Some sharks are as big as an elephant, and some can fit into a small paper bag. Sharks have no bones. They have hundreds of teeth, and when they lose them, they grow new ones. They eat animals of any kind. Whale sharks are the largest of all fish.

Some sharks are as big as ___elephants___.

Sharks have ___hundreds___ of teeth.

___Whale sharks___ are the largest of all fish.

Sharks are fish. True or false? ___True___

Do sharks have bones? ___No___

123

Write a Story

Complete the sentences to write a story about a school trip.

The second-graders went on a trip to _____

The bus ride there was _____

When they arrived, they _____
___Answers will vary.___

Next, they _____

Finally, the class _____

The field trip was _____

124

Write a Story

Write a story about the picture. Describe the characters, setting, and events. Remember to include a beginning, a middle, and an ending.

___Answers will vary.___

125

Write a Story

Plan a story about the picture. Complete the graphic organizer.

Characters
Description:

Description:

Description:

Setting
The story takes place

This place:
looks
sounds
smells

Answers will vary.

Events
The main problem in the story is

The first thing that happens is
The next thing that happens is
The last thing that happens is
The solution to the problem is

126

Write a Story

Use the planner you made on page 126. Write your story below.

Answers will vary.

127

Write to Inform

How do you make a mug of hot chocolate with marshmallows? Complete the sentences to write step-by-step directions.

Hot chocolate is
Answers will vary.

The first step for making hot chocolate is

The next step is

The last step for making hot chocolate is

Enjoy your hot chocolate! Do not forget to

128

Write to Inform

Can you explain how to ride a bicycle? Write step-by-step directions.

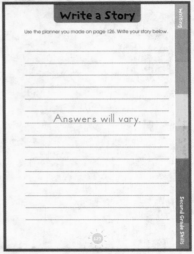

Riding a bicycle is
Answers will vary.

First, you

Then, you

Last, you

With some practice, you will find that riding a bike is

129

Write to Inform

With an adult, do some research to learn facts about the city or state where you live. Complete the sentences.
Answers will vary.
My city/state is

Its geographic size is _____ square miles.

The number of people who live here is

Here are some interesting facts about my city/state:

1.
2.
3.
4.
5.

Complete the luggage tag with **information** about you.

Name
(first)   (last)
Address
City   State   Answers
Phone Number   will vary.
Age

130

Write to Inform

Choose a topic from the list. With an adult, research to learn facts about the topic. Complete the graphic organizer to plan an informative article. Write it on a separate sheet of paper.

| hurricanes | baking | reptiles |
| rain forests | Mt. Everest | U.S. presidents |

My topic is

Introduction:
This topic is interesting or important because
Answers will vary.
Body:

Fact #1:   Fact #2:

Fact #3:   Fact #4:

Conclusion:
The most important thing for readers to remember about my topic is

131

132

Write an Opinion

Circle the statements that give opinions about each topic. Do not circle facts about the topics. To find the opinions, look for judgment words such as **good, better, worst, like,** and so on.

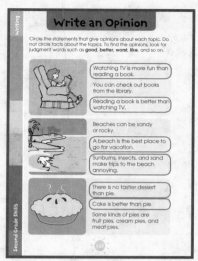

- Watching TV is more fun than reading a book. *(circled)*
- You can check out books from the library.
- Reading a book is better than watching TV. *(circled)*

- Beaches can be sandy or rocky.
- A beach is the best place to go for vacation. *(circled)*
- Sunburns, insects, and sand make trips to the beach annoying. *(circled)*

- There is no tastier dessert than pie. *(circled)*
- Cake is better than pie. *(circled)*
- Some kinds of pies are fruit pies, cream pies, and meat pies.

133

Write an Opinion

What do you think is the best sport to play? Complete the sentence to state your opinion. Then, circle three good reasons for your opinion or write your own reasons.

The best sport to play is _____

Answers will vary.

The reasons I think this are:

It is a team sport.

It is an individual sport.

It is good exercise.

It teaches you important lessons.

You do not need much equipment.

It is played outdoors.

It is played indoors.

It is easy to play.

It is challenging to play.

_____

_____

134

Write an Opinion

What makes a good friend? Complete the first sentence to state your opinion. Then, write three good reasons to support your opinion. Complete the last sentence as a conclusion to your opinion.

The most important way to be a good friend is to

_____
_____.

Reason #1: _____
_____

Reason #2: _____
Answers will vary.

Reason #3: _____
_____

Good friends are _____

135

Write an Opinion

Choose a topic from the list. Then, complete the graphic organizer to plan your writing. Write your complete opinion essay on a separate sheet of paper.

the best way to exercise	the best teacher you've ever had
the best school subject	the best gift you've ever given
the best dinner	the best game to play outside

Introduction:
The best _____ is
_____

Body:
Reason #1: ____ **Answers will vary.**

Reason #2: _____
_____

Reason #3: _____
_____

Conclusion:
Based on the evidence, people should agree with me that _____

136

Add to 20

Add. Do you see a pattern in the sums?

1 + 1 = ②

3 + 1 = ④

2 + 4 = ⑥

4 + 4 = ⑧

8 + 2 = ⑩

6 + 6 = ⑫

8 + 6 = ⑭

9 + 7 = ⑯

10 + 8 = ⑱

10 + 10 = ⑳

137

Subtract Within 20

Subtract. Do you see a pattern in the differences?

20 - 2 = ⑱

17 - 1 = ⑯

19 - 5 = ⑭

18 - 6 = ⑫

15 - 5 = ⑩

16 - 8 = ⑧

18 - 12 = ⑥

19 - 15 = ④

10 - 8 = ②

10 - 10 = ⓪

Answer key

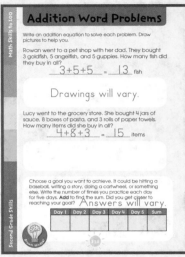

Addition Word Problems

Write an addition equation to solve each problem. Draw pictures to help you.

Rowan went to a pet shop with her dad. They bought 3 goldfish, 5 angelfish, and 5 guppies. How many fish did they buy in all?

$3+5+5 = 13$ fish

Drawings will vary.

Lucy went to the grocery store. She bought 4 jars of sauce, 8 boxes of pasta, and 3 rolls of paper towels. How many items did she buy in all?

$4+8+3 = 15$ items

Choose a goal you want to achieve. It could be hitting a baseball, writing a story, doing a cartwheel, or something else. Write the number of times you practice each day for five days. **Add** to find the sum. Did you get closer to reaching your goal? Answers will vary.

Day 1	Day 2	Day 3	Day 4	Day 5	Sum

138

Subtraction Word Problems

Write a subtraction equation to solve each problem. Draw pictures to help you.

Hayley baked 18 cupcakes. 2 cupcakes fell on the floor. Hayley's sister Kirsten took some cupcakes to her friends outside. Hayley has 11 cupcakes left. How many cupcakes did Kirsten take?

Drawings will vary.

$18-2-11 = 5$ cupcakes

Patrick earned 17 stickers on the reward chart this week. Richard earned 15 stickers. How many more stickers did Patrick earn?

$17-15 = 2$ stickers

Cady and Coen collect marbles. In their collection of 20 marbles, 7 are striped and 4 are swirled. How many marbles are not striped or swirled?

$20-7-4 = 9$ marbles

139

Add to 20

Add from memory.

$\begin{array}{r} 10 \\ +\ 2 \\ \hline 12 \end{array}$ $\begin{array}{r} 6 \\ +\ 7 \\ \hline 13 \end{array}$ $\begin{array}{r} 11 \\ +\ 2 \\ \hline 13 \end{array}$ $\begin{array}{r} 13 \\ +\ 1 \\ \hline 14 \end{array}$

$\begin{array}{r} 16 \\ +\ 4 \\ \hline 20 \end{array}$ $\begin{array}{r} 17 \\ +\ 1 \\ \hline 18 \end{array}$ $\begin{array}{r} 12 \\ +\ 3 \\ \hline 15 \end{array}$ $\begin{array}{r} 1 \\ +\ 1 \\ \hline 2 \end{array}$

$\begin{array}{r} 15 \\ +\ 5 \\ \hline 20 \end{array}$ $\begin{array}{r} 11 \\ +\ 8 \\ \hline 19 \end{array}$ $\begin{array}{r} 5 \\ +\ 5 \\ \hline 10 \end{array}$ $\begin{array}{r} 18 \\ +\ 2 \\ \hline 20 \end{array}$

Being a leader means using your skills to help others. With an adult, lead a collection of gently used clothes to donate to a charity in your community. **Add** the items you collected. Finish the sentence. Answers will vary.

I helped collect _____ items for people in need.

140

Subtract Within 20

Subtract from memory.

$\begin{array}{r} 13 \\ -\ 3 \\ \hline 10 \end{array}$ $\begin{array}{r} 4 \\ -\ 1 \\ \hline 3 \end{array}$ $\begin{array}{r} 5 \\ -\ 2 \\ \hline 3 \end{array}$ $\begin{array}{r} 15 \\ -\ 6 \\ \hline 9 \end{array}$

$\begin{array}{r} 11 \\ -\ 7 \\ \hline 4 \end{array}$ $\begin{array}{r} 19 \\ -12 \\ \hline 7 \end{array}$ $\begin{array}{r} 14 \\ -\ 7 \\ \hline 7 \end{array}$ $\begin{array}{r} 16 \\ -15 \\ \hline 1 \end{array}$

$\begin{array}{r} 15 \\ -\ 4 \\ \hline 11 \end{array}$ $\begin{array}{r} 19 \\ -\ 8 \\ \hline 11 \end{array}$ $\begin{array}{r} 3 \\ -\ 2 \\ \hline 1 \end{array}$ $\begin{array}{r} 14 \\ -10 \\ \hline 4 \end{array}$

$\begin{array}{r} 17 \\ -11 \\ \hline 6 \end{array}$ $\begin{array}{r} 18 \\ -\ 4 \\ \hline 14 \end{array}$ $\begin{array}{r} 16 \\ -\ 4 \\ \hline 12 \end{array}$ $\begin{array}{r} 12 \\ -\ 9 \\ \hline 3 \end{array}$

141

Add & Subtract Within 20

Add or subtract from memory.

$\begin{array}{r} 13 \\ -\ 7 \\ \hline 6 \end{array}$ $\begin{array}{r} 6 \\ +\ 1 \\ \hline 7 \end{array}$ $\begin{array}{r} 8 \\ -\ 3 \\ \hline 5 \end{array}$ $\begin{array}{r} 14 \\ +\ 6 \\ \hline 20 \end{array}$

$\begin{array}{r} 19 \\ -15 \\ \hline 4 \end{array}$ $\begin{array}{r} 15 \\ +\ 2 \\ \hline 17 \end{array}$ $\begin{array}{r} 14 \\ +\ 2 \\ \hline 16 \end{array}$ $\begin{array}{r} 11 \\ -\ 7 \\ \hline 4 \end{array}$

$\begin{array}{r} 8 \\ +\ 8 \\ \hline 16 \end{array}$ $\begin{array}{r} 15 \\ -\ 8 \\ \hline 7 \end{array}$ $\begin{array}{r} 13 \\ -\ 5 \\ \hline 8 \end{array}$ $\begin{array}{r} 18 \\ +\ 2 \\ \hline 20 \end{array}$

$\begin{array}{r} 17 \\ -15 \\ \hline 2 \end{array}$ $\begin{array}{r} 8 \\ +\ 9 \\ \hline 17 \end{array}$ $\begin{array}{r} 14 \\ -\ 9 \\ \hline 5 \end{array}$ $\begin{array}{r} 3 \\ +\ 6 \\ \hline 9 \end{array}$

142

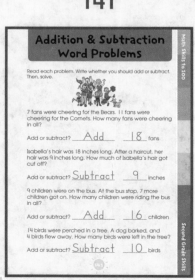

Addition & Subtraction Word Problems

Read each problem. Write whether you should add or subtract. Then, solve.

7 fans were cheering for the Bears. 11 fans were cheering for the Comets. How many fans were cheering in all?

Add or subtract? Add   18 fans

Isabella's hair was 18 inches long. After a haircut, her hair was 9 inches long. How much of Isabella's hair got cut off?

Add or subtract? Subtract   9 inches

9 children were on the bus. At the bus stop, 7 more children got on. How many children were riding the bus in all?

Add or subtract? Add   16 children

14 birds were perched in a tree. A dog barked, and 4 birds flew away. How many birds were left in the tree?

Add or subtract? Subtract   10 birds

143

Answer key

Second Grade Skills

Answer key

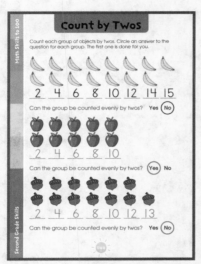

Count by Twos

Count each group of objects by twos. Circle an answer to the question for each group. The first one is done for you.

2 4 6 8 10 12 14 15

Can the group be counted evenly by twos? Yes (No)

2 4 6 8 10

Can the group be counted evenly by twos? (Yes) No

2 4 6 8 10 12 13

Can the group be counted evenly by twos? Yes (No)

144

Count by Twos

Circle pairs in each group of objects. Then, count the objects by twos and answer the questions.

How many pairs did you circle? 3

Can the group be counted evenly by twos? Yes (No)

How many pairs did you circle? 9

Can the group be counted evenly by twos? (Yes) No

How many pairs did you circle? 4

Can the group be counted evenly by twos? Yes (No)

145

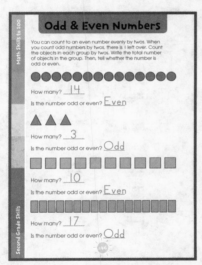

Odd & Even Numbers

You can count to an even number evenly by twos. When you count odd numbers by twos, there is 1 left over. Count the objects in each group by twos. Write the total number of objects in the group. Then, tell whether the number is odd or even.

How many? 14
Is the number odd or even? Even

How many? 3
Is the number odd or even? Odd

How many? 10
Is the number odd or even? Even

How many? 17
Is the number odd or even? Odd

146

Odd & Even Numbers

Color an even number of shapes in each group.

Possible answers shown.

Color an odd number of shapes in each group.

147

Odd & Even Numbers

Color the even numbers orange. Color the odd numbers blue.

1 2 3 4
5 6 7 8
9 10 11 12
13 14 15 16
17 18 19 20

148

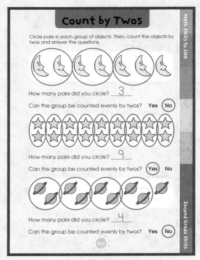

Odd & Even Numbers

Even numbers end with 0, 2, 4, 6, or 8. Odd numbers end with 1, 3, 5, 7, or 9. Circle the even numbers.

16 11 2 30 9

Circle the odd numbers.

15 1 6 20 59

Write your age. Then, write what your age will be in future years. Circle the ages that are **even** numbers. Draw a box around the ages that are **odd** numbers.

Answers will vary.

This year, I am _____ years old.

In 2025, I will be _____ years old.

In 2026, I will be _____ years old.

In 2030, I will be _____ years old.

149

Answer Key

150

Arrays

Look at each group of insects. Write an equation to find the sum of the insects in rows. Then, write an equation to find the sum of the insects in columns. The first one is done for you.

Column

$4 + 4 = 8$
$2 + 2 + 2 + 2 = 8$

$4 + 4 + 4 = 12$
$3 + 3 + 3 + 3 = 12$

$3 + 3 + 3 + 3 + 3 = 15$
$5 + 5 + 5 = 15$

$3 + 3 + 3 = 9$
$3 + 3 + 3 = 9$

151

Arrays

Draw a group of dots to illustrate each pair of addition problems. The first one is done for you.

Rows: $4 + 4 + 4 + 4 + 4 = 20$
Columns: $5 + 5 + 5 + 5 = 20$

Rows: $5 + 5 + 5 + 5 = 20$
Columns: $4 + 4 + 4 + 4 + 4 = 20$

Rows: $3 + 3 = 6$
Columns: $2 + 2 + 2 = 6$

Rows: $5 + 5 + 5 + 5 + 5 = 25$
Columns: $5 + 5 + 5 + 5 + 5 = 25$

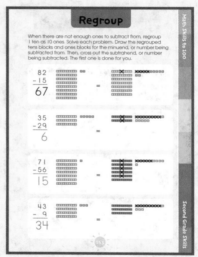

152

Regroup

When the sum of the digits in the ones column is more than 10, regroup 10 ones as 1 ten. Solve each problem. Draw the regrouped tens blocks and ones blocks. The first one is done for you.

$17 + 14 = 31$

$38 + 26 = 64$

$45 + 45 = 90$

$64 + 18 = 82$

153

Regroup

When there are not enough ones to subtract from, regroup 1 ten as 10 ones. Solve each problem. Draw the regrouped tens blocks and ones blocks for the minuend, or number being subtracted from. Then, cross out the subtrahend, or number being subtracted. The first one is done for you.

$82 - 15 = 67$

$35 - 29 = 6$

$71 - 56 = 15$

$43 - 9 = 34$

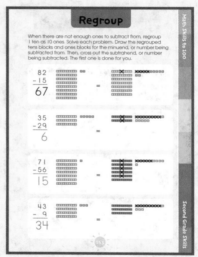

154

Add Two-Digit Numbers

Add. Regroup 10 ones as 1 ten.

$23 + 18 = 41$ $34 + 39 = 73$ $56 + 24 = 80$ $67 + 24 = 91$

$53 + 28 = 81$ $15 + 25 = 40$ $36 + 45 = 81$ $76 + 15 = 91$

$47 + 27 = 74$ $45 + 55 = 100$ $62 + 19 = 81$ $48 + 13 = 61$

$33 + 27 = 60$ $56 + 25 = 81$ $34 + 27 = 61$ $17 + 26 = 43$

155

Addition Word Problems

Read and solve.

Bobby's Bake Shop sold 57 cakes last week. This week, the shop sold 39 cakes. How many cakes did the shop sell during the two weeks?

96 cakes

A farmer has 68 chicken eggs and 24 duck eggs. How many eggs does the farmer have in all?

92 eggs

Finley has two apple trees in her backyard. One tree has 42 apples. The other tree has 38 apples. How many apples are on the trees in Finley's backyard?

80 apples

Work with a partner. Think about what the two of you have in common. The ideas below will get you started. Add all the things you have in common and write the sum.

Answers will vary.

pets   friends   favorite sports
families   toys   favorite foods
hobbies   interests   favorite movies

We have _____ things in common!

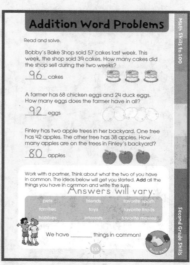

Answer Key

Subtract Two-Digit Numbers

Subtract. Regroup 1 ten as 10 ones.

82 −69 **13**	73 −36 **37**	25 −17 **8**	76 −37 **39**
88 −19 **69**	58 −39 **19**	27 −18 **9**	57 −18 **39**
37 −27 **10**	71 −56 **15**	36 −18 **18**	40 −21 **19**
51 −24 **27**	36 −27 **9**	82 −44 **38**	62 −15 **47**

156

Subtraction Word Problems

Read and solve.

28 students in Sam's class played Bingo on a rainy day. 19 of those students won a prize. How many students did not win a prize?

___9___ students

Ms. Taylor scooped 45 scoops of ice cream for the children at her son's birthday party. At the end of the party, 16 scoops had not been eaten. How many scoops of ice cream were eaten?

___29___ scoops

Bryn took a walk around the pond. She saw 14 frogs and 34 birds. On her second loop around the pond, she counted 19 birds. How many birds had flown away?

___15___ birds

To be a good listener, do four things: look into the person's eyes, lean slightly forward, nod and say things like "uh-huh," and ask questions. Ask a friend to talk while you do all these things. Then, one by one, **subtract** each behavior. How does your friend feel each time? Take turns to see how you feel when someone is and is not a good listener.

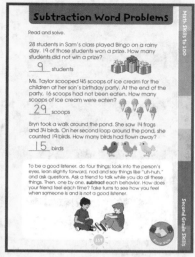

157

Add & Subtract Two-Digit Numbers

Add or subtract. Regroup as needed.

41 +56 **97**	90 −45 **45**	76 +12 **88**	59 −34 **25**
95 −63 **32**	43 +17 **60**	82 −56 **26**	63 −40 **23**
68 −29 **39**	32 +33 **65**	51 +19 **70**	69 −47 **22**
76 −30 **46**	57 −19 **38**	67 +20 **87**	86 +11 **97**

158

Addition & Subtraction Word Problems

Read each problem. Write whether you should add or subtract. Then, solve.

One fawn weighs 54 pounds. Her brother weighs 43 pounds. How much do they weigh in all?

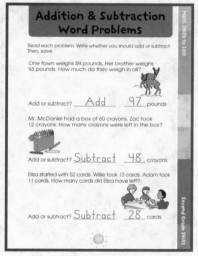

Add or subtract? __Add__ __97__ pounds

Mr. McDaniel had a box of 60 crayons. Zac took 12 crayons. How many crayons were left in the box?

Add or subtract? __Subtract__ __48__ crayons

Eliza started with 52 cards. Willie took 13 cards. Adam took 11 cards. How many cards did Eliza have left?

Add or subtract? __Subtract__ __28__ cards

159

Place Value

A number with three digits is made up of ones, tens, and hundreds. In the number 234, 4 is in the ones place. Its value is 4 ones, or 4. The digit 3 is in the tens place. Its value is 3 tens, or 30. The digit 2 is in the hundreds place. Its value is 2 hundreds, or 200. Write the number shown by each group of hundreds, tens, and ones blocks. The first one is done for you.

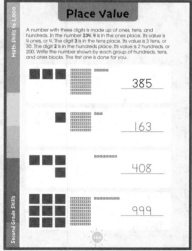

	385
	163
	408
	999

160

Place Value

Write the number shown by each group of hundreds, tens, and ones blocks.

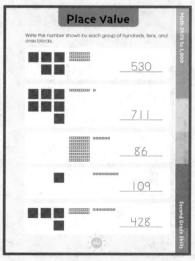

	530
	711
	86
	109
	428

161

Answer key

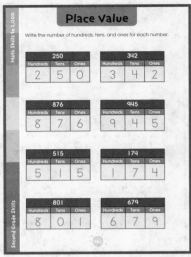

162

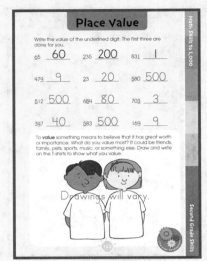

163

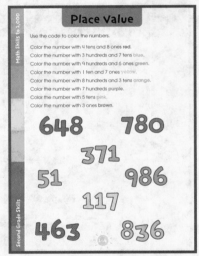

164

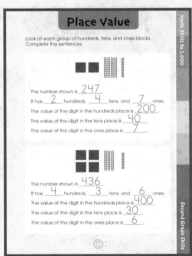

165

Expanded Form

Expanded form is a way to write a number by adding the values of its digits. Look at each number. Complete its expanded form. The first one is done for you.

823
800 + 20 + 3

567
500 + 60 + 7

680
600 + 80 + 0

409
400 + 0 + 9

166

Expanded Form

Look at each expanded form. Circle the matching number.

500 + 80 + 6
(586)
568
580

200 + 30
203
233
(230)

400 + 10 + 2
410
(412)
421

900 + 50 + 7
907
(957)
975

800 + 4
840
(804)
844

70 + 5
705
750
(75)

Look at each number. Circle its expanded form.

363 — 300 + 30 + 6 — (300 + 60 + 3) — 300 + 63 + 0

913 — 900 + 13 — 900 + 30 + 1 — (900 + 10 + 3)

619 — (600 + 10 + 9) — 61 + 9 — 600 + 90 + 1

167

Expanded Form

Write each number in expanded form.

144	100 + 40 + 4
460	400 + 60
73	70 + 3
347	300 + 40 + 7
675	600 + 70 + 5
68	60 + 8
942	900 + 40 + 2
473	400 + 70 + 3
999	900 + 90 + 9

168

Expanded Form

Complete the chart.

Standard Form	Expanded Form
84	80 + 4
921	900 + 20 + 1
635	600 + 30 + 5
866	800 + 60 + 6
99	90 + 9
612	600 + 10 + 2
709	700 + 9
228	200 + 20 + 8

169

Number Names

Match the numbers and words.

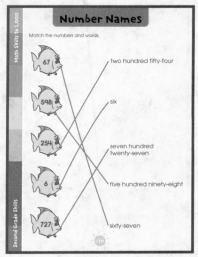

67 — sixty-seven
598 — five hundred ninety-eight
254 — two hundred fifty-four
6 — six
727 — seven hundred twenty-seven

two hundred fifty-four

six

seven hundred twenty-seven

five hundred ninety-eight

sixty-seven

170

Number Names

Cut out the numbers. Tape or glue them in the boxes to complete the chart.

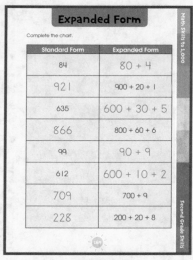

	Hundreds	Tens	Ones
two hundred seventy-eight	2	7	8
four hundred twenty-three	4	2	3
five hundred seventeen	5	1	7
six hundred fifty-eight	6	5	8
one hundred thirty-six	1	3	6
nine hundred forty-nine	9	4	9

171

Number Names

Write the name of each number. Do not use the word **and**. If the number has 2 or more tens and more than 0 ones, use a hyphen (-) between the words that name them. The first two are done for you.

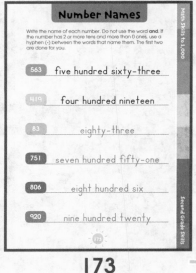

563	five hundred sixty-three
419	four hundred nineteen
83	eighty-three
751	seven hundred fifty-one
806	eight hundred six
920	nine hundred twenty

173

Write Numbers Three Ways

Complete the number pyramids. The first one is done for you.

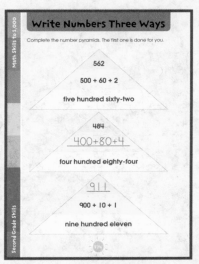

562
500 + 60 + 2
five hundred sixty-two

484
400 + 80 + 4
four hundred eighty-four

911
900 + 10 + 1
nine hundred eleven

174

Write Numbers Three Ways

Complete the number pyramids.

804
800+4
eight hundred four

668
600 + 60 + 8
six hundred sixty-eight

779
700 + 70 + 9
seven hundred seventy-nine

175

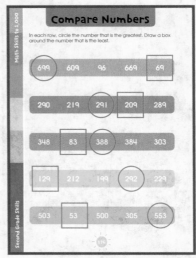

Compare Numbers

In each row, circle the number that is the greatest. Draw a box around the number that is the least.

699 609 96 669 69

290 219 291 209 289

348 83 388 384 303

129 212 199 292 229

503 53 500 305 553

176

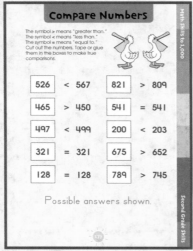

Compare Numbers

The symbol > means "greater than."
The symbol < means "less than."
The symbol = means "equal to."
Cut out the numbers. Tape or glue them in the boxes to make true comparisons.

526 < 567   821 > 809

465 > 450   541 = 541

497 < 499   200 < 203

321 = 321   675 > 652

128 = 128   789 > 745

Possible answers shown.

177

Compare Numbers

Write <, >, or = in each circle.

366 < 929   581 > 259   928 > 172

163 < 642   545 > 501   445 < 466

600 + 40 + 8 < six hundred fifty-eight

800 + 70 + 7 > 800 + 7

900 + 20 + 7 = 900 + 20 + 7

one hundred fifty-five > 100 + 50 + 1

six hundred eighty-seven > 600 + 70 + 8

179

Count by Ones

Count forward and backward by ones from the numbers shown. Write the missing numbers.

699 700 701 702 703

315 316 317 318 319

569 570 571 572 573

996 997 998 999 1,000

180

Count by Fives

Count forward and backward by fives from the numbers shown. Write the missing numbers.

440 445 450 455 460

285 290 295 300 305

810 815 820 825 830

980 985 990 995 1,000

181

Answer key

Count by Tens

Count forward and backward by tens from the numbers shown. Write the missing numbers.

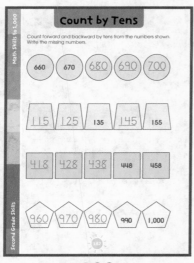

| 660 | 670 | 680 | 690 | 700 |

| 115 | 125 | 135 | 145 | 155 |

| 418 | 428 | 438 | 448 | 458 |

| 960 | 970 | 980 | 990 | 1,000 |

182

Count by Hundreds

Count forward and backward by hundreds from the numbers shown. Write the missing numbers.

| 300 | 400 | 500 | 600 | 700 |

| 250 | 350 | 450 | 550 | 650 |

| 316 | 416 | 516 | 616 | 716 |

| 599 | 699 | 799 | 899 | 999 |

183

Number Patterns

Decide if each pattern shows counting by ones, fives, tens, or hundreds. Write the missing numbers.

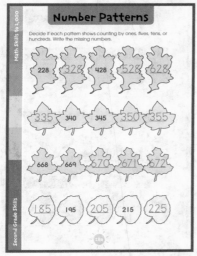

| 228 | 328 | 428 | 528 | 628 |

| 335 | 340 | 345 | 350 | 355 |

| 668 | 669 | 670 | 671 | 672 |

| 185 | 195 | 205 | 215 | 225 |

184

Number Patterns

Decide if each pattern shows counting by ones, fives, tens, or hundreds. Write the missing numbers.

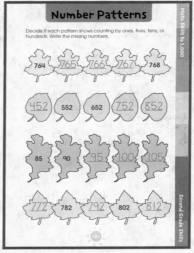

| 764 | 765 | 766 | 767 | 768 |

| 452 | 552 | 652 | 752 | 852 |

| 85 | 90 | 95 | 100 | 105 |

| 772 | 782 | 792 | 802 | 812 |

185

Add & Subtract 10

Add 10 to each number. Use the number in the tens place to help you. It is **red**.

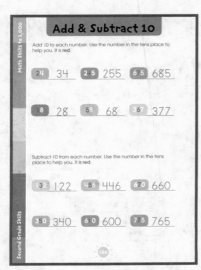

24 34   245 255   675 685

8 28   58 68   367 377

Subtract 10 from each number. Use the number in the tens place to help you. It is **red**.

32 122   456 446   670 660

350 340   610 600   775 765

186

Add & Subtract 10

Look at each number. Write the numbers that are 10 more and 10 less.

| −10 | +10 | | −10 | +10 |
| 324 | 334 | 344 | 68 | 78 | 88 |

| −10 | +10 | | −10 | +10 |
| 516 | 526 | 536 | 841 | 851 | 861 |

| −10 | +10 | | −10 | +10 |
| 635 | 645 | 655 | 259 | 269 | 279 |

187

305

Answer key

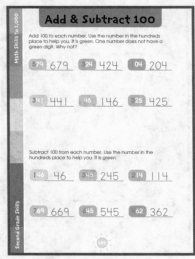

188

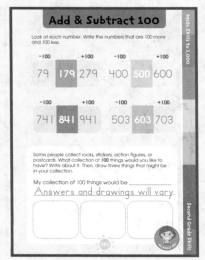

189

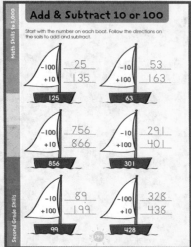

190

191

192

Add Two-Digit Numbers

Add. Color the matching sums on the flag.

55	56	68	32	79
30	41	90	35	51
+78	+36	+10	+89	+79
163	133	168	180	306

12	71	87	96	56
45	53	54	35	41
78	84	42	25	38
+69	+62	+78	+70	+72
204	270	261	226	207

168	514	133	328
840	306	609	226
163	206	180	145
302	204	840	207
270	708	261	908

193

306

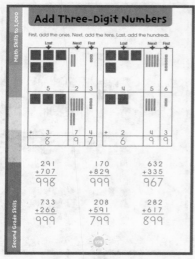

194

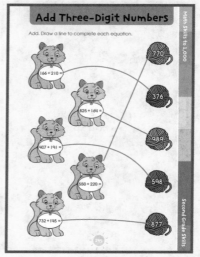

195

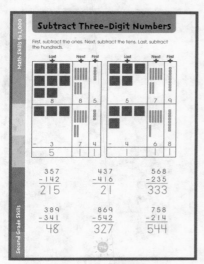

196

Subtract Three-Digit Numbers

Subtract. Draw a line to complete each equation.

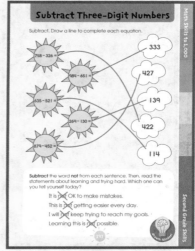

Subtract the word **not** from each sentence. Then, read the statements about learning and trying hard. Which one can you tell yourself today?

It is not OK to make mistakes.

This is not getting easier every day.

I will not keep trying to reach my goals.

Learning this is not possible.

197

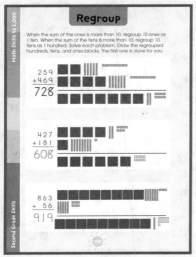

198

Add Three-Digit Numbers

Add. Regroup 10 ones as 1 ten. Regroup 10 tens as 1 hundred. Two are done for you.

258	425	744
+467	+489	+207
725	914	951

423	734	642
+257	+149	+319
680	883	961

152	536	437
+348	+128	+268
500	664	705

523	366	618
+427	+235	+349
950	601	967

199

Second Grade Skills

Add Three-Digit Numbers

Add. Write the missing numbers.

$$\begin{array}{r} ①13 \\ +25⑨ \\ \hline 372 \end{array} \qquad \begin{array}{r} 215 \\ +5②7 \\ \hline 74② \end{array} \qquad \begin{array}{r} 124 \\ +53⑧ \\ \hline ⑥62 \end{array}$$

$$\begin{array}{r} 194 \\ +6⑤8 \\ \hline ⑧52 \end{array} \qquad \begin{array}{r} ③54 \\ +349 \\ \hline 70③ \end{array} \qquad \begin{array}{r} 323 \\ +347 \\ \hline ⑥70 \end{array}$$

$$\begin{array}{r} 214 \\ +⑥58 \\ \hline 87② \end{array} \qquad \begin{array}{r} 67④ \\ +138 \\ \hline 8①2 \end{array} \qquad \begin{array}{r} ②23 \\ +765 \\ \hline 98⑧ \end{array}$$

200

Regroup

When there are not enough ones to subtract from, regroup 1 ten as 10 ones. When there are not enough tens to subtract from, regroup 1 hundred as 10 tens. Solve each problem. Draw the regrouped hundreds blocks, tens blocks, and ones blocks for the minuend, or number being subtracted from. Then, cross out the subtrahend, or number being subtracted. The first one is done for you.

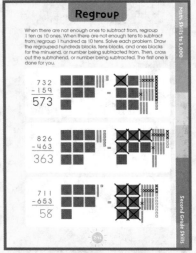

$$\begin{array}{r} 732 \\ -159 \\ \hline 573 \end{array}$$

$$\begin{array}{r} 826 \\ -463 \\ \hline 363 \end{array}$$

$$\begin{array}{r} 711 \\ -653 \\ \hline 58 \end{array}$$

201

Subtract Three-Digit Numbers

Subtract. If needed, regroup 1 ten as 10 ones. Regroup 1 hundred as 10 tens. Follow the example.

$$\begin{array}{r} \tiny 11 \\ 5\cancel{1}7 \\ \cancel{6}\cancel{2}7 \\ -459 \\ \hline 168 \end{array}$$

1. Subtract the ones. 9 ones cannot be subtracted from 7 ones. Regroup 1 ten as 10 ones: 17 – 9 = 8. Only 1 ten is left.
2. Subtract the tens. 5 tens cannot be subtracted from 1 ten. Regroup 1 hundred as 10 tens: 11 – 5 = 6. Only 5 hundreds are left.
3. Subtract the hundreds: 5 – 4 = 1.

$$\begin{array}{r} 832 \\ -627 \\ \hline 205 \end{array} \qquad \begin{array}{r} 475 \\ -228 \\ \hline 247 \end{array} \qquad \begin{array}{r} 597 \\ -459 \\ \hline 138 \end{array}$$

$$\begin{array}{r} 638 \\ -219 \\ \hline 419 \end{array} \qquad \begin{array}{r} 944 \\ -635 \\ \hline 309 \end{array} \qquad \begin{array}{r} 383 \\ -267 \\ \hline 116 \end{array}$$

$$\begin{array}{r} 347 \\ -239 \\ \hline 108 \end{array} \qquad \begin{array}{r} 932 \\ -703 \\ \hline 229 \end{array} \qquad \begin{array}{r} 861 \\ -102 \\ \hline 759 \end{array}$$

202

Subtract Three-Digit Numbers

Subtract. Regroup as needed. Use the code to color the flowers.

If the difference has 1 one, color it **red**.
If the difference has 5 ones, color it **yellow**.
If the difference has 7 ones, color it **purple**.
If the difference has 8 ones, color it **pink**.

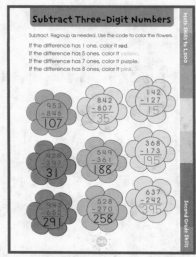

$$\begin{array}{r} 953 \\ -846 \\ \hline 107 \end{array} \qquad \begin{array}{r} 842 \\ -807 \\ \hline 35 \end{array} \qquad \begin{array}{r} 142 \\ -127 \\ \hline 15 \end{array}$$

$$\begin{array}{r} 428 \\ -397 \\ \hline 31 \end{array} \qquad \begin{array}{r} 549 \\ -361 \\ \hline 188 \end{array} \qquad \begin{array}{r} 368 \\ -173 \\ \hline 195 \end{array}$$

$$\begin{array}{r} 943 \\ -652 \\ \hline 291 \end{array} \qquad \begin{array}{r} 528 \\ -270 \\ \hline 258 \end{array} \qquad \begin{array}{r} 637 \\ -242 \\ \hline 395 \end{array}$$

203

Add & Subtract Three-Digit Numbers

Add or subtract. Regroup when needed.

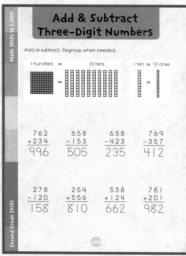

| 1 hundred | = | 10 tens | 1 ten | = | 10 ones |

$$\begin{array}{r} 762 \\ +234 \\ \hline 996 \end{array} \quad \begin{array}{r} 658 \\ -153 \\ \hline 505 \end{array} \quad \begin{array}{r} 658 \\ -423 \\ \hline 235 \end{array} \quad \begin{array}{r} 769 \\ -357 \\ \hline 412 \end{array}$$

$$\begin{array}{r} 278 \\ -120 \\ \hline 158 \end{array} \quad \begin{array}{r} 254 \\ +556 \\ \hline 810 \end{array} \quad \begin{array}{r} 538 \\ +124 \\ \hline 662 \end{array} \quad \begin{array}{r} 781 \\ +201 \\ \hline 982 \end{array}$$

204

Addition & Subtraction Word Problems

Read and solve.

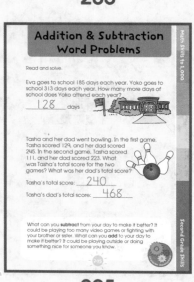

Eva goes to school 185 days each year. Yoko goes to school 313 days each year. How many more days of school does Yoko attend each year?

___128___ days

Tasha and her dad went bowling. In the first game, Tasha scored 129, and her dad scored 245. In the second game, Tasha scored 111, and her dad scored 223. What was Tasha's total score for the two games? What was her dad's total score?

Tasha's total score: ___240___

Tasha's dad's total score: ___468___

What can you **subtract** from your day to make it better? It could be playing too many video games or fighting with your brother or sister. What can you **add** to your day to make it better? It could be playing outside or doing something nice for someone you know.

205

Answer Key

Measure in Inches

Look at the kangaroo's foot. It is three inches long. Use a ruler to measure the length of each animal's foot to the nearest inch.

2 inches

1 inch

1 inch

3 inches

206

Measure in Inches

Estimate the length of each object in inches. Then, use a ruler to measure each object to the nearest inch.

	Estimated Length	Actual Length
your foot		
your hand		
toothbrush		
fork	Answers will vary.	
drinking glass		
paper clip		
your shoe		

Try to touch your toes without bending your knees. If you cannot reach your toes, ask a friend to use a ruler to measure how many more **inches** you still need to stretch. Practice for five days. Then, measure again. Did you become more flexible and get closer to your goal?

207

Inches & Feet

Most rulers are one foot long. There are 12 inches in one foot. Write **inches** or **feet** below each object to tell whether you would measure its length in inches or in feet.

inches

inches

feet

inches

feet

inches

feet

feet

208

Measure in Centimeters

A centimeter measures length in the metric system. There are about two and one-half centimeters in one inch. Look at the kangaroo's foot. It is eight centimeters long. Find a ruler that has centimeters. Use it to measure the length of each animal's foot to the nearest centimeter.

8 centimeters

2 centimeters

3 centimeters

3 centimeters

209

Measure in Centimeters

Estimate the length of each object in centimeters. Then, use a ruler to measure each object to the nearest centimeter.

	Estimated Length	Actual Length
your foot		
your hand		
toothbrush		
fork	Answers will vary.	
drinking glass		
paper clip		
your shoe		

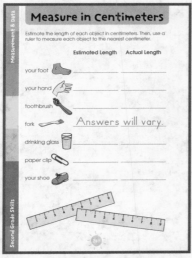

210

Centimeters & Meters

There are 100 centimeters in one meter. Write **centimeters** or **meters** beside each object to tell whether you would measure its length in centimeters or in meters.

meters

meters

centimeters

centimeters

meters

meters

centimeters

meters

211

Answer key

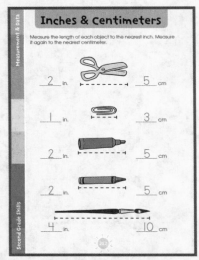

212

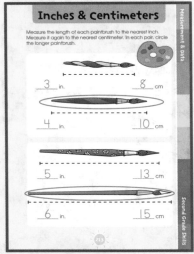

213

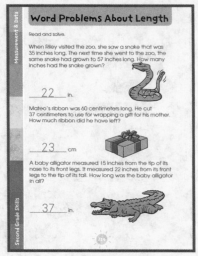

214

215

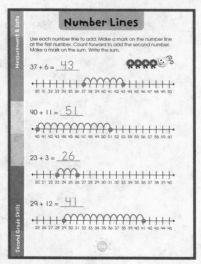

216

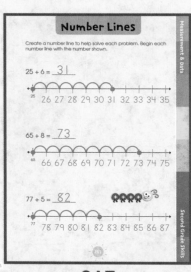

217

Answer Key

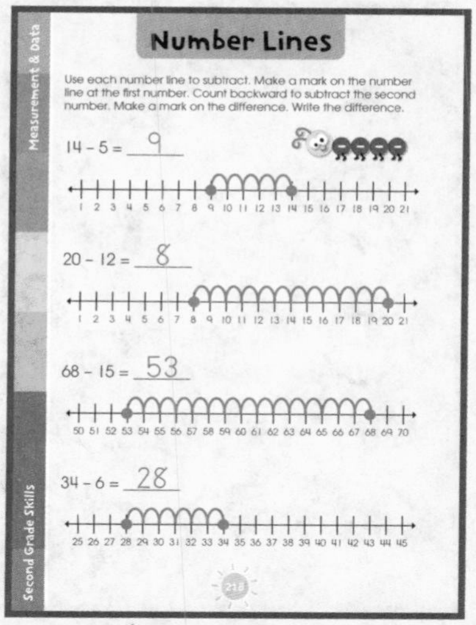

Number Lines

Measurement & Data

Use each number line to subtract. Make a mark on the number line at the first number. Count backward to subtract the second number. Make a mark on the difference. Write the difference.

14 − 5 = 9

20 − 12 = 8

68 − 15 = 53

34 − 6 = 28

Second Grade Skills

218

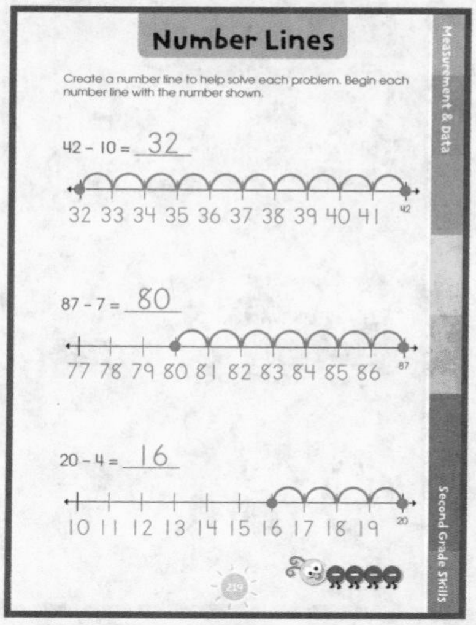

Number Lines

Measurement & Data

Create a number line to help solve each problem. Begin each number line with the number shown.

42 − 10 = 32

32 33 34 35 36 37 38 39 40 41 42

87 − 7 = 80

77 78 79 80 81 82 83 84 85 86 87

20 − 4 = 16

10 11 12 13 14 15 16 17 18 19 20

Second Grade Skills

219

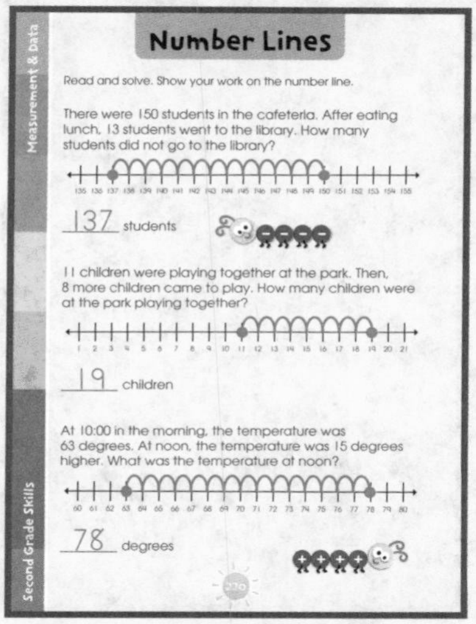

Number Lines

Measurement & Data

Read and solve. Show your work on the number line.

There were 150 students in the cafeteria. After eating lunch, 13 students went to the library. How many students did not go to the library?

137 students

11 children were playing together at the park. Then, 8 more children came to play. How many children were at the park playing together?

19 children

At 10:00 in the morning, the temperature was 63 degrees. At noon, the temperature was 15 degrees higher. What was the temperature at noon?

78 degrees

Second Grade Skills

220

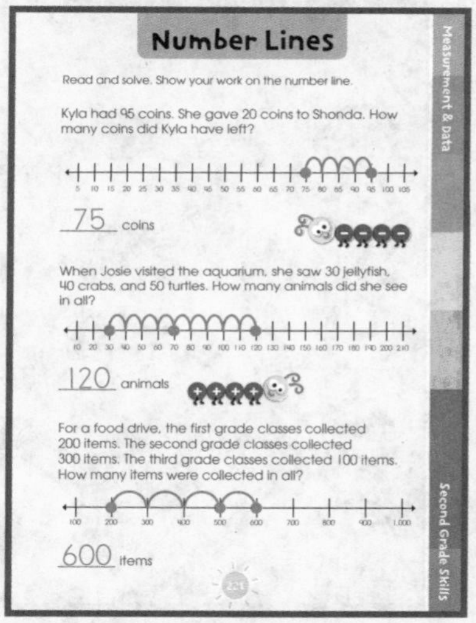

Number Lines

Measurement & Data

Read and solve. Show your work on the number line.

Kyla had 95 coins. She gave 20 coins to Shonda. How many coins did Kyla have left?

75 coins

When Josie visited the aquarium, she saw 30 jellyfish, 40 crabs, and 50 turtles. How many animals did she see in all?

120 animals

For a food drive, the first grade classes collected 200 items. The second grade classes collected 300 items. The third grade classes collected 100 items. How many items were collected in all?

600 items

Second Grade Skills

221

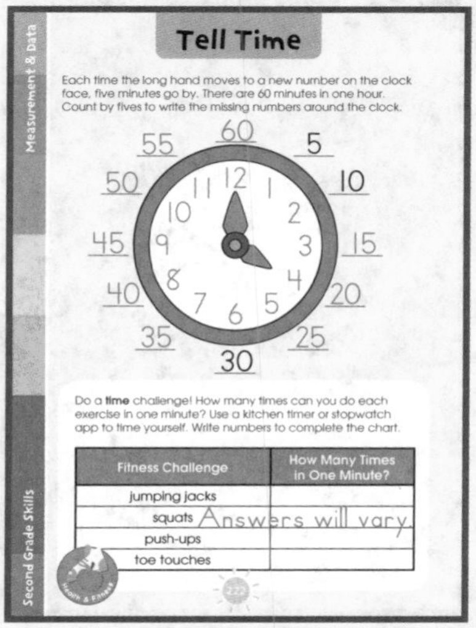

Tell Time

Measurement & Data

Each time the long hand moves to a new number on the clock face, five minutes go by. There are 60 minutes in one hour. Count by fives to write the missing numbers around the clock.

Do a **time** challenge! How many times can you do each exercise in one minute? Use a kitchen timer or stopwatch app to time yourself. Write numbers to complete the chart.

Fitness Challenge	How Many Times in One Minute?
jumping jacks	
squats	Answers will vary.
push-ups	
toe touches	

Second Grade Skills

222

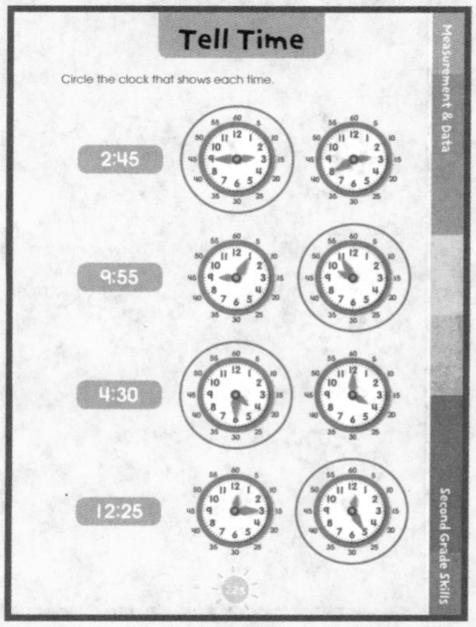

Tell Time

Measurement & Data

Circle the clock that shows each time.

2:45

9:55

4:30

12:25

Second Grade Skills

223

Answer Key

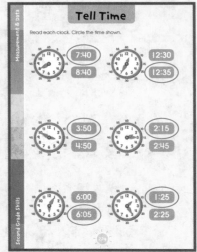

224

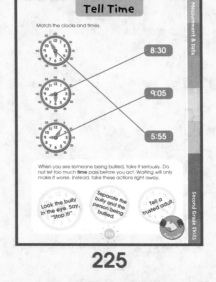

225

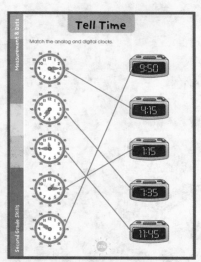

226

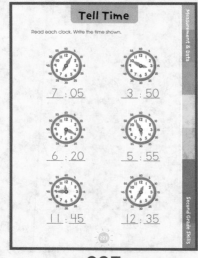

227

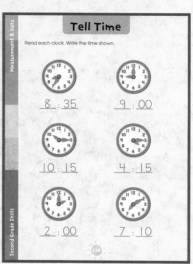

228

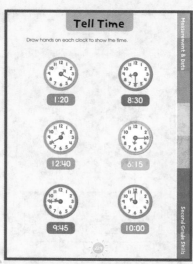

229

230

231

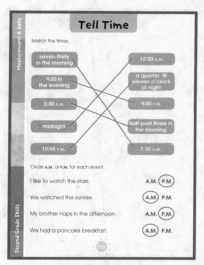

232

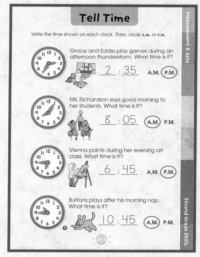

233

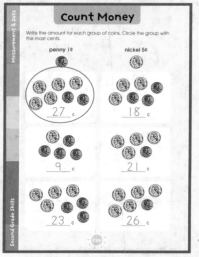

234

Count Money

Count the coins and write the total amount. Circle the group with the most cents.

penny 1¢   nickel 5¢   dime 10¢

37 ¢   34 ¢

43 ¢   64 ¢

20 ¢   46 ¢

235

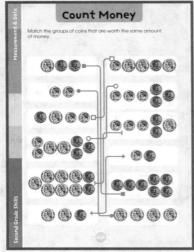

236

Measurement & Data
Second Grade Skills

237

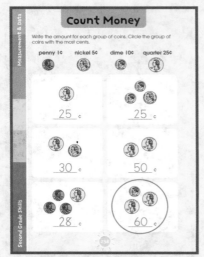

238

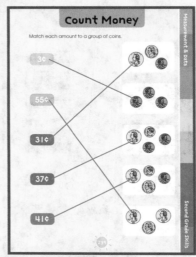

239

240

241

Answer key

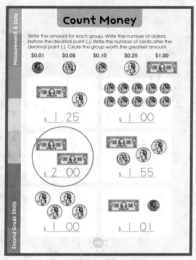

242

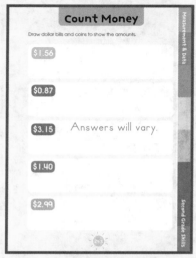

243

244

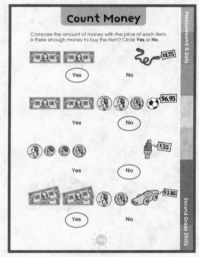

245

246

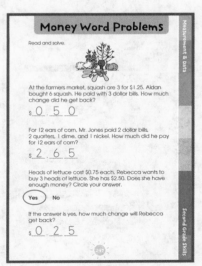

247

315

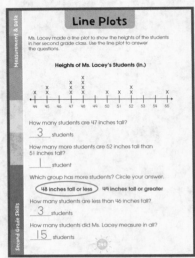

248

Line Plots

Ms. Lacey made a line plot to show the heights of the students in her second grade class. Use the line plot to answer the questions.

Heights of Ms. Lacey's Students (in.)

How many students are 47 inches tall?
___3___ students

How many more students are 52 inches tall than 51 inches tall?
___1___ student

Which group has more students? Circle your answer.
(48 inches tall or less)   49 inches tall or greater

How many students are less than 46 inches tall?
___3___ students

How many students did Ms. Lacey measure in all?
___15___ students

249

Line Plots

During one afternoon outside, Devin found eight creatures and measured their lengths. Make a line plot to show Devin's data. Draw an **X** above the line plot for each creature.

1 in.   1 in.   2 in.

6 in.

1 in.   3 in.   2 in.

Length of Creatures Found in Devin's Backyard (in.)

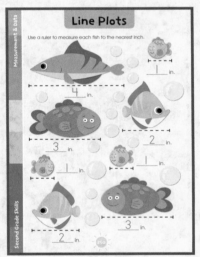

250

Line Plots

Use a ruler to measure each fish to the nearest inch.

1 in.

4 in.

3 in.   2 in.

1 in.   1 in.

3 in.

2 in.

251

Line Plots

Use the data you collected on page 250 to make a line plot. For each fish, draw an **X** above the line to show its measurement. Then, answer the questions.

Length of Fish (in.)

How many fish are 2 inches long?
___2___ fish

How many more fish are 1 inch long than 3 inches long?
___1___ fish

How many fish are 2 inches long or longer?
___5___ fish

How many fish did you measure in all?
___8___ fish

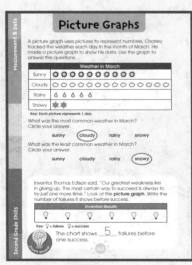

252

Picture Graphs

A picture graph uses pictures to represent numbers. Charley tracked the weather each day in the month of March. He made a picture graph to show his data. Use the graph to answer the questions.

Weather in March	
Sunny	☀☀☀☀☀☀☀☀☀
Cloudy	☁☁☁☁☁☁☁☁☁☁☁
Rainy	💧💧💧💧💧
Snowy	❄❄

Key: Each picture represents 1 day.

What was the most common weather in March? Circle your answer.
sunny   (cloudy)   rainy   snowy

What was the least common weather in March? Circle your answer.
sunny   cloudy   rainy   (snowy)

Inventor Thomas Edison said, "Our greatest weakness lies in giving up. The most certain way to succeed is always to try just one more time." Look at the **picture graph**. Write the number of failures it shows before success.

Invention Results					

Key: 💡 = failure   💡 = success

The chart shows ___5___ failures before one success.

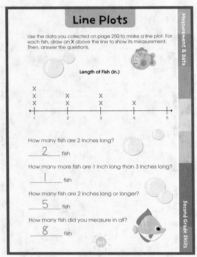

253

Picture Graphs

Cady owns a cupcake shop. She made a picture graph to show how many cupcakes she sold each day for a week. Use the graph to answer the questions. Notice that each picture in the graph stands for more than one cupcake.

Cady's Cupcake Sales in One Week	
Monday	🧁🧁🧁🧁🧁🧁🧁🧁🧁🧁
Tuesday	🧁🧁🧁
Wednesday	🧁🧁🧁
Thursday	🧁🧁🧁🧁🧁🧁🧁
Friday	🧁🧁🧁🧁🧁🧁🧁🧁🧁🧁🧁

Key: 🧁 = 5 cupcakes

On Wednesday, Cady sold 15 cupcakes. Draw this data in the graph.

On which day did Cady sell the most cupcakes?
___Friday___

How many cupcakes did Cady sell on Monday?
___50___ cupcakes

How many more cupcakes did Cady sell on Thursday than on Tuesday? ___20___ cupcakes

How many cupcakes did Cady sell this week?
___185___ cupcakes

Answer key

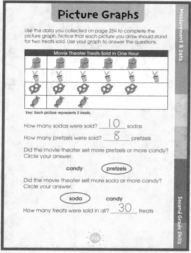

255

256

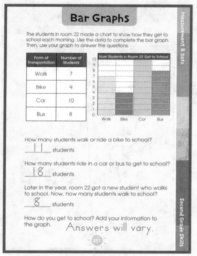

257

Bar Graphs

Use the data you collected on page 258 to complete the bar graph. Then, use your graph to answer the questions.

How many watermelons and lemons are for sale?
___7___ watermelons and lemons

How many more pears are for sale than lemons?
___3___ pears

How many pieces of fruit does Giuseppe have in all?
___23___ pieces of fruit

259

260

Quadrilaterals

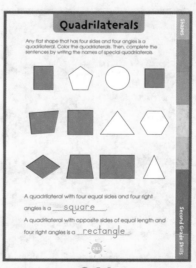

A quadrilateral with four equal sides and four right angles is a ___square___

A quadrilateral with opposite sides of equal length and four right angles is a ___rectangle___

261

Answer Key

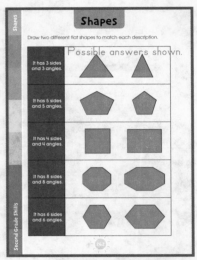

262

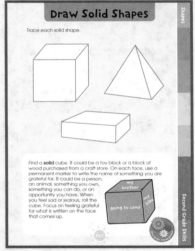

265

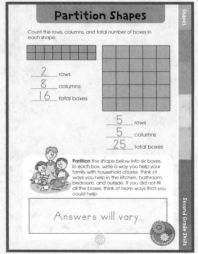

267

263

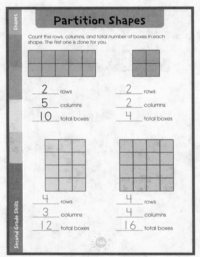

266

268

Answer Key

Second Grade Skills

Answer key

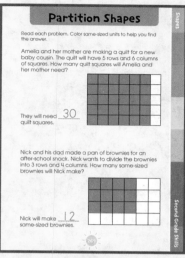

269

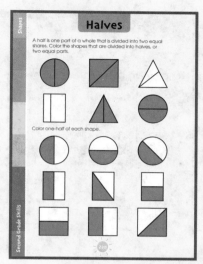

270

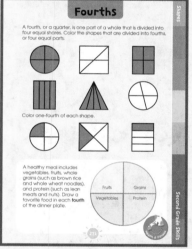

271

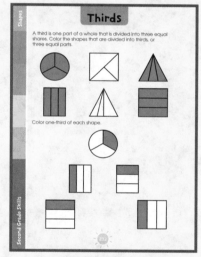

272

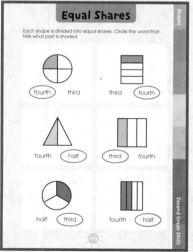

273

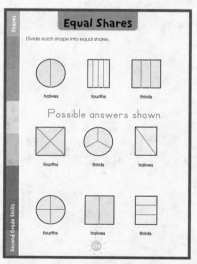

274

319

Answer key

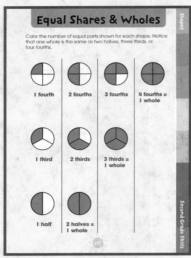

275